50 Checklists

for project
and programme managers

Rudy Kor and Gert Wijnen

Gower   Twynstra

Management Consultants

© Twynstra Management Consultants 2000

Published by

Gower Publishing Limited	Gower
Gower House	Old Post Road
Croft Road	Brookfield
Aldershot	Vermont 05036
Hampshire GUI I 3HR	USA
England	

R. Kor and G. Wijnen have asserted their right under the Copyright, Designs and Patents Act 1988 to be identified as the authors of this work.

British Library Cataloguing in Publication Data
Kor, R.
Fifty checklists for project and programme managers
1   Industrial project management
I   Title   II   Wijnen, G.
658.4'04

ISBN   0-566-08278-0

Designed and typeset
Jo Bovendorp and Sjoukje Ziel
(Twynstra Management Consultants)

Photography
Jan van IJken

Illustrations
Jan Zandstra

Printed by
Cambridge University Press, Great Britain

Contents

Foreword

Since the 1970's, the Twynstra Group of Managers and Consultants, of which we are partners, has dedicated itself to the professionalisation of project-based working. This approach has its roots in the construction industry, as do so many other management approaches that still characterise the field today.

Our approach soon became 'common property'; this came about by our close association with the computer and software industry, which at that time was in its infancy, but also the electronics industry and our continual involvement in organisation change processes.

This approach has been made suitable for both capital-intensive and capital-deficient projects, for projects where only a few people are involved to projects with an army of full-time workers. It has been adapted for projects that have a tangible end result, but also for projects that are more at home in the world of ideas. The disadvantage of this is that the approach is not really tailored to any one specific type of project. This is left up to the reader!

About 15 years ago, the complexity of certain assignments made us realise that, as well as the project approach, we needed a new one. We called this the programme approach, which is characterised by aiming towards goals instead of results.

Culture counts

From its beginnings as a small Dutch bureau in the 1960's, Twynstra has grown into an organisation employing more than 700 people who work in offices spread all over Europe. After all these years, we are convinced that the approaches we have developed are effective within the Dutch culture.

We have seen that our methods have helped in the management of unique assignments in northern Europe. We have to qualify this by mentioning that our approach, quite obviously, contains elements specific to our culture and therefore limitations, for example in relation to power differences. These must not be too great between the principal and the assignment leader, otherwise you will lose the all-important consultation moments and the relationship will become hierarchical, within which any criticism from the assignment leader will be regarded as a form of insubordination.

The 'mañana' attitude of some cultures does not exactly stimulate a more planned approach to working; nor does the absolute belief, held by a decreasing number of cultures, that planning is not the way forward.

Too much ego tripping does a project or programme no good at all; it must be a team effort. But having a team where conflicts are not aired is no good either, because there will always be conflict situations in the course of a unique assignment. After all, there may be no common interests or well-trodden paths to fall back on.

Why should you not read this book?
Many unique assignments can be carried out using the management method par excellence: Intuition, with the motto: We Will Wait And See What Happens. If you are happy with this approach, it will not really be worth your time while reading this book. You will probably gain more insight and inspiration from books such as De Bono's on the subject of thinking, *Alice in Wonderland*, Murphy's Law, Baron von Münchhausen and the *The Tao of Poeh*.

This book is also not the book of choice for people wanting a scientific foundation to the project and programme approach. It is too practically oriented for this purpose.

If you are looking for budget calculation methods, execution period calculation models, comparative studies of software packages or the latest information about coaching team members, you would be better advised to put this book to one side, since these subjects are not covered.

If you have absolutely nothing to do with a project or programme at this time, the book will certainly add to your general knowledge, but it is designed as a handbook and not a work of scientific interest, so your time might be better employed on something else.

Why should you read this book?
This book is aimed at people who, in one way or another, are involved or are about to become involved in a project or programme.

If your organisation works systematically, but you have the feeling that this could be improved, the book will offer you suggestions. If you have any doubts about the suitability of your own systematic way of working or feel that it could be improved, this book might help you address these questions.

It makes no difference when reading this book if you work for a profit or non-profit organisation, in an organisation that makes products or one that provides services. It is also immaterial if you work in an organisation with a staff of 222 or one employing 22.222. Systematic working can have its place in all types of organisations. It also makes no difference whether you are male or female; to avoid elegance we use he in this book to indicate he or she.

The book can be read from cover to cover, but you could also choose to read about a particular theme, such as working together. You could also concentrate on the checklists and skip the introductory texts, but you would miss the context in which they are placed. Or you can just read the introductory texts, but if you do you will miss the practicality that so typifies the checklists.

This book is complete in itself. However, it would be remiss of us if we did not refer to the book *Managing Unique Assignments*, a publication that takes a closer look at the six themes dealt with here. It has a similar list of contents, but rather than being a practical handbook, *Managing Unique Assignments* lays the foundations for the project and programme approach.

It still remains a time-consuming busginess
The project or programme approach spares those involved a great deal of inconvenience. But this does not say that there is nothing to it. Because a unique assignment always involves bringing staff together temporarily, it is a time-consuming business. Time and time again, agreements have to be made with capacity suppliers about the division of tasks, responsibilities and powers.

We must be careful to avoid turning a construction that has been used successfully in one unique assignment into the standard for all the subsequent ones.

Organisations that want to approach unique assignments in a professional way must be willing to reach new tailor-made agreements for each individual case. Clear use of language helps in this by making communication easier.

It is also useful to know what has to be done at any given time, thus avoiding the necessity of starting from scratch. Our intention is to help you on your way; what you actually say and do are up to you.

Amsterdam, September 1999
Rudy Kor and Gert Wijnen

Unique assignments

People in organisations are regularly confronted with new situations that they have no answer to: a customer wants something new, the government introduces new legislation or the competition brings something new on to the market. Other causes lie within the organisation itself. Someone senses a new opportunity, a new product or service is developed or a new policy has to be implemented.

Projects and programmes are characterised by their temporary nature, which makes it virtually impossible to fall back on existing tools. Unique assignments; such as developing an information campaign, improving customer orientation, the development and introduction of new legislations, increasing market share, compiling a brochure for a foundation, obtaining an ISO certificate, introducing a new computer system, reducing feelings of uncertainty and introducing a patient follow-up system; cannot be carried out using previously determined standard procedures. They are also usually too important to tackle using an improvised approach. These assignments, regarded by those concerned in the organisation as important, contain many new elements, making it impossible for people to fall back on previous experience and methods.

Unique assignments in organisations

Some organisations - such as architects, automation, engineers, research and consulting bureaux, but also comparable (support) departments - owe their existence to repeatedly carrying out other people's unique assignments.

Other organisations are formed temporarily to carry out just one major assignment, only to be disbanded when that assignment is completed. Yet other organisations exist merely to produce exactly the same product or deliver precisely the same services year in, year out. This type of organisation is characterised by routine processes, strictly defined tasks and everyone knowing exactly what their job is. This does not mean that the organisation cannot be confronted by new unique assignments, however. Imagine, if you will, the development of a new coffee machine, the introduction of a new information system or the carrying out of a major reorganisation. Project management, and in certain cases programme management, are useful tools for achieving these ends. But before looking at this in more detail, we will begin by looking at other recognised work forms.

There are various possible approaches to working, of which improvisation and routine - seldom to be found in their pure form - can be considered the extremes on a sliding scale (see Figure 1.1).

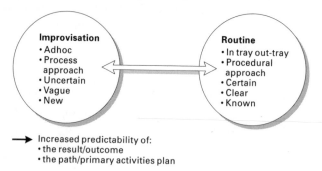

1.1   Different approaches to working

Routine work is characterised by repetition: both the result and the activities necessary to achieve it are predictable, because this is not the first time that 'something like this' has been carried out. A routine approach is most suitable if a particular result must be achieved repeatedly under identical circumstances and with identical resources. The most important advantage of the routine approach is the possibility of achieving efficacy.

Improvisation scores low on repetition. Where flexibility is concerned, the methods are diametrically opposed: flexibility is the strength of improvisation. This approach typically goes with 'novel' actions, with both unpredictable activities and/or results. Improvisation is often inevitable if you do not know the outcome of the work that has to be done. An improvisational approach to a problem is most logical if an entirely new activity is involved, which has to be carried out under new circumstances.

The project approach and the programme approach are hybrid forms. Depending on the nature of the problem, the situation and the preferences of the employees who will have to carry out the actual work, the characteristics of the various work forms can be positively or negatively valued. It is important that those involved recognise how the work is being approached, because they will have to adjust their management of it accordingly.

Basic principles in the management of unique assignments

To be able to carry out projects and programmes, people will have to work together in ways that they have never done before. They will have to make unique agreements about how they will work together. Someone who is just a member of staff can suddenly find himself in the role of project leader.

In organisations where many projects are being carried out simultaneously, the same person can be a member of the project team in one project, project leader in another and project secretary in yet another. This puts him in a variety of positions with his direct bosses and colleagues. Agreements are necessary to regulate these different relationships.

Project and programme management are useful tools for managers and staff, enabling them to direct each other's efforts and energy towards achieving a project result and strive for the goals in a programme. Those working in projects or programmes are offered a new perspective, one that makes the why and the wherefore of the work clearer and more easily communicable for everyone.

Only when a direction has been determined and a plan been drawn up can the activities be controlled and managed. The project and programme approach also provides the necessary jargon, rules of the game and tools to do this. In the language of projects and programmes, managing is always aimed towards the future. Plans are an essential means of communication. Using a plan as a tool of progress control means: 'Now, at this time, we agree to the following. We will all stick to the plan, but the most important aspect is that if we think that we will have to deviate from it, we will only do so if the decision has been a joint one.' In this way, when necessary, the plan will be reliably revitalised, adjusted and changed without people ever losing sight of the result and goals being pursued.

It is important to give explicit attention to the decision making process of unique assignments. When making decisions on routine matters the organisation can fall back on formal and informal procedures, but projects and programmes are unique. The people involved have never before carried out these activities in this field with this combination of people. By definition, in each new project and each new programme the decision will have to be taken as to who decides what and what the consequences of this decision will be.

Projects and programmes
The unique assignments highlighted most in this book are projects and programmes. Both these types of collective activities, the one result oriented and the other goal oriented, do not exist as such.
Projects or programmes can be 'made' from a collection of activities that have to produce a unique result,

or pursue a unique set of goals, respectively. Calling a number of activities a project or a programme is a conscious choice. There are some people who never get any further than this. They continue to work in the same old way and only call something a project or a programme to give it priority over other activities. Others realise and accept the consequence that choosing to work in this way really means working differently.

Concerning projects

A project is a unique complex of activities aimed at achieving a jointly predetermined, unique result that must be realised with limited means. This definition contains two key concepts, both of which must be wholly or partially new and unique: result and activities. The most important of these is the result that must be achieved. The work necessary to do this is of secondary importance. This speaks for itself, because if the result that is aimed for is not clear, it is already a waste of time and effort making an inventory of these activities, let alone starting them.

The project approach is made up of three linked parts: phasing, managing and decision making. Each part is aimed at making the end result even clearer and prompting co-operation between the parties involved. In our interpretation, this begins with describing as clearly as possible the 'why' (the goals to be pursued or the problems to be deminished), the 'what' (that which is completed, when it is completed) and the work that will be carried out in the various phases and the 'how' (the way in which time, money, quality, information and organisation are managed). The third component of this approach is decision making; deciding at the end of each phase if you agree with what has been done and whether the work yet to be carried out is worthwhile.

Concerning programmes

Whereas the aim of a project is the realisation of a previously determined result, a programme pursues multiple, sometimes even conflicting goals. This means that project management is fundamentally different from managing a programme.

A programme is a unique complex of goal-oriented efforts, including projects, which must be carried out with limited means. The key concepts in this definition are efforts and goal orientation.

In this context, efforts, activities, primary activities and the method of execution are all synonymous. Routines, improvisations and projects are all efforts that could be equally at home in a programme. The number of projects is usually very low during the start-up stage, increases during the implementation stage, only to decrease again in the shutdown stage. Improvisations are mostly found in the start-up stage and routines become freely available in the implementation and shutdown stages.

The programme approach is made up of three closely linked elements: programming, management and decision making. Each of these elements is designed to achieve previously determined effects (intended goals) and promote co-operation between those involved.

But there is common ground: both projects and programmes concentrate on directing and bundling the energy of those involved and defining the various roles and rules of the game as clearly as possible. The theme of each part of this approach is to define the end result or end goals with increasing clarity (directing and bundling energy!) and to promote and simplify co-operation between the parties involved. In addition, although they are not identical, both make use of planning and progress-control procedures. In both approaches, attention has to be paid to environmental factors and players, and these have to be mapped out for each individual assignment. For every player involved, it is important to identify what his interest in the assignment is and how he views it.

But when all is said and done, the realisation of an assignment stands or falls by the co-operation of the people involved in it: their ability and desire to work together constructively and their willingness to recognise conflicts and solve them harmoniously.

The project approach

Project management is a specific set of management techniques, aimed at achieving a result by means of a project and at managing all project activities from the very start through to the very end. Over the past few decades, more and more managers have come to recognise that the project approach is an effective and efficient method for implementing special assignments. Unfortunately, many of those who use these techniques often do so in an unconsciously fragmented and sometimes uninformed way.

This chapter deals with the vocabulary and the basics of the project approach. This approach is based on our consulting and managing experience over the last 30 years in the field of project management in different situations such as organisation renewal, the housing and building process, policy formulation and the development and implementation of information systems. Though these projects certainly differ one from another, there are common issues in their management. The project approach being discussed can be applied to internal projects, product development, relocation etc., as well as external projects carried out for outside clients, supplying systems, implementing mergers, executing studies, building offices and roads.

In short, a project-based approach requires:
- those involved to recognise that 'routine' tasks need to be managed differently from special or 'one-off' assignments;
- not just calling an assignment a project, but also managing it accordingly, accepting the idea that projects do not exist as such: they are 'created' by the people involved. They must make sure that the project is of the relevant nature and will be executed accordingly;
- one person to act as the project principal. This greatly simplifies management and decision making;
- a list of activities and a sequence (phases) in which these activities are to be carried out;

- continuous progress-control of the five management aspects: time, money, quality, information and organisation;
- integration, in a decision document, of the outcome of the previous phase with the forecast of the activities that have to be done in the next phase(s) and the (adjusted) management plans for the five management aspects;
- taking decisions based on a decision document at the end of each phase, opting for continuation or termination of the project;
- the early involvement of the project manager and project team, because the sooner they are involved, the more committed they will be to the implementation of the project.

From the idea to the description of the result

A project needs an owner. Sometimes this function is called sponsor, client or user, but a better word is principal. The best principal is a person who wants to solve a problem or who sees an opportunity that cannot be passed up. Good principals experience both the joys and the sorrows of a project. They are the ones who can anticipate the consequences of choices and who are going to do something with its result.

For a project to succeed, it is essential that all parties who participate in one way or another in the project want to achieve the same result (see Figure 2.1). Other words to describe what is meant by 'result' are product, deliverable, solution, means or output.

Clarification of the issues, problems or goals is one of the activities needed to arrive at a result description. This requires empathy on the part of the project manager and openness on the part of the principal. The principal must be willing to make information available. In addition, he must be prepared to state his own goals, aspirations and ambitions. Some principals do not like this at all and feel that project managers should just do as they are told. But projects require extra effort from project managers. They should be able to commit themselves to the project, to believe in it and to feel that it is feasible. By examining the context in which the project is to be realised, the project manager gains insight into the various forces surrounding the project at hand. A project's feasibility depends on two aspects: a technical aspect - is the necessary knowhow present? - and a social aspect - will those involved, such as staff members, line management and society at large, allow the result to be produced?

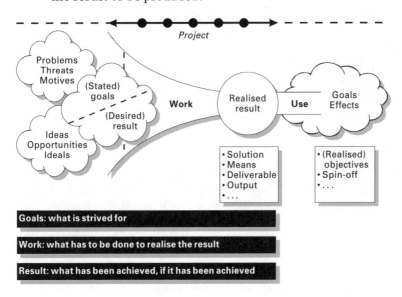

2.1   A project is result oriented

Phasing the project

The result description is the basis for an inventory of the *primary activities* that need to be carried out. You need to identify all the activities that have to be done between start and completion of the project. Each and every one of these activities must be assigned to a particular phase (Figure 2.2). As we shall see later, phasing is necessary for planning and progress controlling of the actual project.

Phasing a project helps you with structured decision making and it reduces uncertainty because it makes progress visible. Phasing means grouping related tasks together. Each phase must be treated equally, not so much in terms of time or in required resources but definitely in terms of importance. Each transition between phases is a logical point for the principal to make the decision either to continue or to discontinue the project.

Dividing a project into six phases will reduce even the most complex projects to activities and tasks that can be planned and executed with confidence. Later, you will see that this is the foundation for the management of the project.

The *initiative phase* of a project is the only one that does not have a clearly defined beginning. By the end of this phase, the project result must be known and the way in which this result is to be achieved must be determined (whether via a project approach or in some other way).

The *definition phase* is when the project is specified in terms of external interfaces, functional and operational requirements and in design constraints. This phase answers the question: 'What should the result perform?'

In the *design phase*, the project takes concrete form in terms of chosen solutions that are acceptable in terms of the project requirements. The phase answers the question: 'What should the result look like?'

In the *preparation phase*, everything required during the actual realisation of the project is made ready and available. Designs are organisationally as well as technically prepared by means of, for example, production planning, production process descriptions, training programmes, job instructions and so on. In this phase, you want to ensure that implementation can take place smoothly 'by just pressing a button'.

In the *realisation phase*, the project is finally implemented, carried out or built in accordance with the requirements.

In the *follow-up phase*, the project is used, maintained and, if necessary, modified. The primary activities in this phase are using the realised project, maintaining the realised project and maintaining tools, aids and resources. This phase is not a part of the project as such, it is only prepared by the project team. The owner of the project executes the work that has to be done.

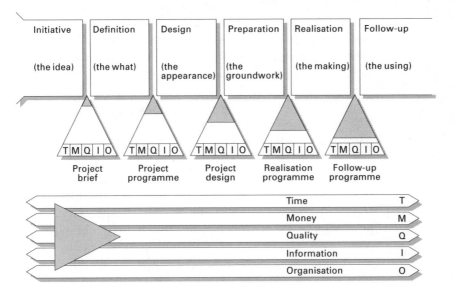

2.2   The project approach integrates phasing, managing and decision making

Managing the project

Planning and progress controlling of time, money, quality, information and organisation are continuous activities throughout the project. Phasing the project helps you both in finding out what primary activities have to be done and in doing them. Planning and progress controlling the project will enable you to ensure that the project will be executed according to plan. To this end, five questions concerning the five management aspects need to be answered.

For all five aspects the following have to be clear:
– What is the management requirement (standard, norm, plan) including its margins?
– Who is responsible for controlling progress and how often should this be done?
– How are data to be processed in a progress report?
– Who is authorised to make adjustments (within and outside the set margins)?

Time: Have the beginning and end dates of the project been set and have the related number of man-hours and materials been determined?

Important tasks in the planning of time are estimating the total leadtime, detailing this leadtime for each activity to be carried out, and relating all necessary project activities to calendar time. When this has been done, the necessary resources for each activity have to be allocated. The last activity is getting all schedules approved and issued to all concerned.

Finance: Is there a budget, thus making it clear what the project may cost and what the expected returns are?

Important tasks for the planning of money are estimating the total expenditures and revenues for the project, detailing the costs for each activity to be carried out, placing all expected expenditures/revenues in calendar time, obtaining approval of all preliminary calculations, cashflow, estimates and budget schedules and issuing the approved financial schedules and budgets to all concerned.

Quality: Is it clear how good the result must be and how this is to be proved? Quality management in a project is about ensuring that the project conforms to the quality requirements stated, by demanding controllable, measurable criteria and conducting the planned quality control tests. Quality in a project means the extent to which the project result satisfies the quality requirements (good is good enough).

Important tasks for the planning of quality control are specifying quality requirements for the project result, and ensuring that all these requirements can be controlled in one way or another.

Information: Are there any procedures for drawing up, releasing, changing and distributing baseline or decision documents?

Important tasks for the planning of information control are identifying which information needs to be controlled, deciding on a decision document coding system and determining who must release which decision document, who must receive which decision document, via whom which decision document must be transmitted, and in what form and where, how and by whom which decision document must be filed and can be changed.

Organisation: Have all relevant organisational structures been laid down, such as principalship, project management, project team composition, division of tasks, responsibilities and powers and lines of communication? Does everybody know how decisions are to be made?

Important tasks in the planning of organisation are ensuring that powers, tasks and responsibilities are unambiguously assigned, defining the formal channels of communication such as meetings, setting up both formal and informal decision-making processes, getting teams and individuals within the project functioning operationally, setting up formal networks for communication and relationships between the project organisation and its environment.

These five management aspects must be sufficiently attuned to one another. For example, it would be totally inappropriate to spend a great deal of energy on scheduling while neglecting quality management. It is also important to recognise that the different management aspects do not influence each other. Adding additional funds to a project will not necessarily decrease leadtimes.

Decision making

During the entire project, choices and decisions must be made continuously. Various levels of decision making can be distinguished. For example, a decision must be made as to whether to start the project and what priority it should have. Senior management usually makes such external decisions. After all, they have an overview of, and insight into, the long-term development of the organisation and can therefore judge whether and how a project fits into this picture.

Then a large number of decisions are made during each phase, such as who to interview, what methods or technique to use or how to keep those involved informed. Such decisions are made by the project manager and the project team members.

In our approach to project management, the most important decisions are those that are made at the end of each phase, on whether or not to continue the project. The project principal - possibly in consultation with senior management and the stakeholders - is responsible for these decisions.

To aid him in making these decisions systematically, he has decision documents. These are also often known as basline documents, contract, tender, plan, proposal, task description, milestone, offering, consolidation document and agreement.

In making decisions at the transition of one phase to the next, it is important to avoid having to reverse earlier decisions too often or too easily. At the same time, these decisions should not unnecessarily limit the project's line of development. The nature of the decisions that principals need to make is therefore linked to the project's current phase (see Figure 2.3).

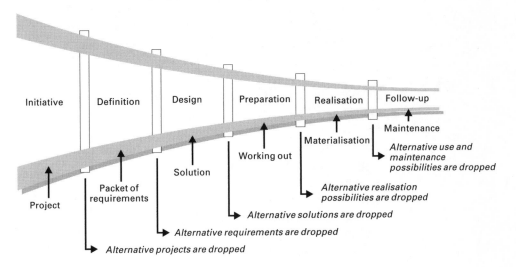

2.3   Decisions in a project

Decision documents serve to integrate and record the outcome of the previous phase(s). The documents also specify what needs to be done in the subsequent phase(s), how much time this will take, what financial consequences this will have, how the quality of the results are to be reported and adjusted and what everyone's tasks, powers and responsibilities are. In that sense, the document looks ahead. As soon as the principal has approved the decision document's contents, it becomes a contract: the basis for the next phase.

Hence, a decision document is not just a *conclusion* of the previous phase, it is also a *starting point* for the next one. Through this document, the project manager has a contract with the principal about the result to be achieved, the work necessary to achieve it and the related agreements concerning the planning and progress control of the project. Decisions to be made during the phase or phases that fall within this contract can be made by the project manager personally.

The principal must be notified about any imminent deviations from the contract during or at the end of the phase.

In order to ensure consistency of the phase-concluding or decision documents, they must all be structured in the same way, to include:
– a description of the project result to be achieved, in as much as this can be deduced on the basis of the phase activities;
– a description of planned primary activities. These are described in detail for the next phase and more generally for the later phases;
– a description of the state of affairs concerning the five management aspects; their planning and progress control (who controls progress, how and how often, and who adjusts and replans, and how?).

In addition to functioning in the formal sense described above, a decision document also works as an important means of communication. The regular exchange of ideas at the end of each phase allows ideas about the project, and the attending expectations as to what will and will not be realised, to be brought into line. This also prevents the project from becoming a concern for the project team only.

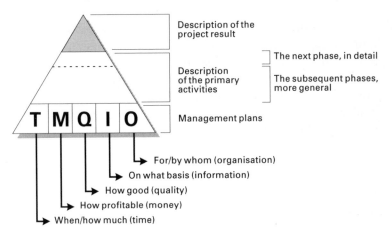

One way to ensure that the project principal stays committed and continues to feel responsible is to inform him regularly about the project's progress. At the very least, this should be done during the transition from one phase to the next. In this way - and this is very important - it will enable the principal to prove that he is responsible, since he has a tool at this disposal, namely the decision documents.

Summary

A project-based approach saves all those involved a great deal of inconvenience. But that does not mean that the project runs itself. Because it always requires a temporary combination of human resources, it consumes a great deal extra time and energy from all involved.

For every project, separate - and often different - agreements must be reached with the capacity suppliers about the division of powers and responsibilities and the way in which the project is being reported to the permanent organisation. Therefore, managers of an organisation must realise that the organisation can only implement a limited number of projects at the same time.

But good project management can help to complete unique, costly and complex, resuly-oriented assignments that involve complex and numerous tasks, deadlines and continual communication across organisational boundaries. Above all, with professional project management, working on a project will be a learning experience for all those involved.

2.1 Turn it into a project

A project consists of a number of activities that will be carried out in a controlled way with limited means to reach a unique result. The tools used to facilitate the project approach will be discussed later. These are divided into primary tools, management tools and tools to aid decision making.

Not everything that is called a project is actually a project that can or should be tackled as such. A project-based method of working is only possible when a project meets certain preconditions. Only then is it worth implementing this method of working and a controlled procedure is possible. Ensure that the project has an adequate number of characteristics found in the 'ideal' project.

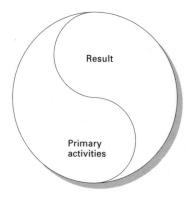

The ideal project:
- has a defined beginning and end
- is result oriented
- is unique
- is multidisciplinary
- is complicated
- is uncertain
- is costly
- is essential to those concerned
- can be controlled from one point
- has one principal or client.

The specification of the project content is made up of two parts: the description of the intended project result, and the plan of approach, primary activities or steps necessary to achieve this result. The result specification becomes clearer as the project progresses. It will be most concrete at the end of the realisation phase where the realised result is specified. The plan of approach is always most detailed for the phase about to be started and more global for later phases.

Usually a number of people are involved in a project, often including some from other departments. It is not uncommon to have several people from different organisations involved in the same project. This often makes the specification of the project content absorbing and difficult. Indeed, all these people have their own very different language for and experience of a project approach. But at the end of the day, the project content must mean the same thing to all those concerned.

A project has to be made

Project pitfalls:

- When the project result is a goal, the problem or intended effect is formulated: e.g. a cleaner country, more customer-friendly personnel.
- The result description is too vague: e.g. an optimal intranet.
- It is not said what the result is *not*.
- In principle, people only negotiate from a base of conflicting interests.
- Conflicting demands are accepted in the hope that they will go away or not be as bad as was feared.

1 Checklist

Determine the project result

A project starts by determining what it has to produce. As long as this has not been sufficiently and clearly determined, carrying out any kind of primary activities is a very risky business. A good result specification is the basis of a good plan of approach. The project result must be determined beforehand.

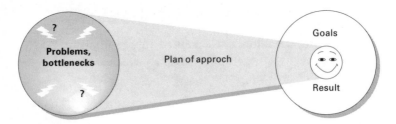

The project result may be a tangible as well as an intangible object

How to achieve this:

- Determine the intentions, expectations and opinions of all those involved in the project.
- List those parts of the goals that can be achieved and the possible consequences if they are not.
- Describe the relevant problems and bottlenecks in the current situation or those expected in the near future and, where possible, back them up with facts and figures.
- List those parts of the problems or bottlenecks that can be solved and the possible consequences if the intended contribution does not materialise.
- Ensure that everyone involved regards the project as being sufficiently important, making it possible to push it through.
- Give a global, unambiguous description of the project's end result, with special emphasis on what does not belong to it.

A number of tips:

- A project result is *what has been achieved when the project is finished.*
- The description of the project result contains only nouns and a great many adjectives. There are *no* verbs.
- The project result is that which can later be proved to exist: a product, a thing, a deliverable, the output, the system, the accommodation, an analysis report, a book, a working organisation etc.

2.1.2 Phase the project

Only when the result of the project has been sufficiently determined and defined can thoughts turn to the primary activities that have to be implemented to achieve this result and the sequence in which they should be carried out. These primary activities are laid down in a plan of approach. However, this should not be a straitjacket. Based on current insights and the situation as it now stands, it should only give an indication of how the project can best be carried out. A plan of approach is always more detailed for today than for the day after. Insights and circumstances are continually changing and so must the plan of approach, but always in a controlled way and never implicitly.

Initiative	Definition	Design	Preparation	Realisation	Follow-up
(the idea)	(the what)	(the appearance)	(the groundwork)	(the making)	(the using)

In each phase, the primary work for the forthcoming phase will have to be detailed as well as roughly setting out the work for all the remaining phases

Phase	Aim
Initiative	Consider what the project result should and should not be; all those involved have the same picture
Definition	Consider exactly what the project result should be or do (requirements/wishes/performance)
Design	Consider what the project result should look like: a detailed complete solution, a design
Preparation	Consider how the project result should be made, what it will look like: by pressing a button the required project result will appear
Realisation	The carrying out or introduction of the project result: making it tangible
Follow-up	Using, upkeeping and maintaining the project result

The project activities are described by active verbs

How to achieve this:

– Consider all the primary activities necessary for achieving the project result.
– Consider these activities in sequence, from beginning to end but also from the end to the beginning.
– Do this together with those who will actually be carrying out the work.
– Determine the natural/logical order for carrying out these activities.
– Determine which activities could be carried out in parallel, possibly by splitting up some.
– Make sure that the description of each activity contains an active verb.
– Where appropriate, describe what the interim result of an activity should be.
– Specify the tools, materials, approach or method necessary for each activity.

A number of tips:

– A plan of approach contains only primary activities, not managerial ones.
– If a project contains a large number of activities, dividing these activities into constituent projects can be useful.
– The plan of approach contains not only the fun activities or those of the project team but all the primary activities needed to achieve the project result.

Carry out the initiative phase

The initiative phase is concerned with acquiring an even-handed description of the indication and size of the project and its result from all those concerned. On completion of this sometimes long-drawn-out process, it should be possible to answer the following questions:

- Why this project? – the pursued goals and/or the problems to be addressed.
- What should the result be? – the result in general terms.
- What should the result not be? – the boundaries.

Initiative	Definition	Design	Preparation	Realisation	Follow-up
(the idea)	(the what)	(the appearance)	(the groundwork)	(the making)	(the using)

Well begun is half done

How to achieve this:

- Record the general state of affairs.
- Investigate the global problems or goals.
- Formulate the desired result.
- Investigate the basic feasibility and enforceability of the critical elements in particular.
- Define the provisional boundaries of the project.
- Draw up the plan of approach; in this case, describe the primary activities in each phase in the correct order:
- a detailed description of the definition phase, where necessary describing how these activities will be tackled
- a more general description for the remaining phases.
- Set up the primary part of the project brief.

A number of tips:

- Making a good start is always half the battle.
- Almost everything that goes wrong during a project has its origins in the initiative phase.
- There is never enough time to carry out the initiative phase properly the first time around, but always enough to repeat it over and over again.

Carry out the definition phase

The definition phase is aimed at putting together a concrete package of requirements for the intended project result in terms of external interfaces, functional requirements (required performance), operational requirements and design constraints. What exactly do we expect from the project result?

Initiative	Definition	Design	Preparation	Realisation	Follow-up
(the idea)	(the what)	(the appearance)	(the groundwork)	(the making)	(the using)

For those who don't know the what, every how is a solution

How to achieve this:

– Gather together the basic material.
– Determine the project requirements:
· external interfaces
· functional requirements
· operational requirements
· design constraints.
– Investigate the feasibility of the requirements and eliminate those that are not feasible.
– Eliminate conflicting requirements.
– Draw up the plan of approach; in this case, detail and adjust the overview of the primary activities for each phase in the correct order:
· a detailed description of the design phase, where necessary describing how these activities will be tackled
· a more general description for the remaining phases.
– Set up the work structure and define the constituent projects and the relationship between them.
– Set up the primary part of the project programme.

A number of tips:

– Avoid vague requirements.
– It is better to have a heated discussion about conflicting requirements now than putting this off until a later phase.
– A forgotten external interface will always have dramatic consequences.

Carry out the design phase

The design phase is aimed at putting together a completed, detailed solution/design of the project result. What will the detailed project result look like?

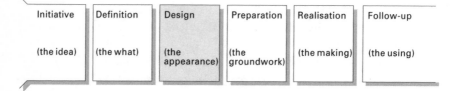

Initiative	Definition	Design	Preparation	Realisation	Follow-up
(the idea)	(the what)	(the appearance)	(the groundwork)	(the making)	(the using)

It's not about how you tackle the project, but how the project result will look

How to achieve this:

- Detail the project programme.
- Investigate 'make or buy' possibilities.
- Look for solutions for or design each constituent project.
- Look for or design project tools.
- Gear constituent project solutions to project tools.
- Adjust the constituent designs when they have been checked, tested or tried out.
- Draw up the definite, detailed project design for:
- the constituent projects
- the tools.
- Draw up the plan of approach; in this case, detail and adjust the overview of the primary activities for each phase in the correct order:
- a detailed description of the preparation phase, where necessary describing how these activities will be tackled
- a more general description for the remaining phases.
- Set up the primary part of the project design.

A number of tips:

- The 'what' determines the 'how', rather than vice versa.
- A good design can be made, used, maintained ... and demolished.
- Prevent the designers tinkering endlessly with the design: it has to be completed at some stage.

Carry out the preparation phase

The preparation phase is geared to gaining an exact description of the aimed for project result thus ensuring its smooth realisation, at the press of a button.

Initiative	Definition	Design	Preparation	Realisation	Follow-up
(the idea)	(the what)	(the appearance)	(the groundwork)	(the making)	(the using)

To get it right first time requires foresight

How to achieve this:

- Work out the detailed design in realisation diagrams, production plans, production lists etc.
- Draw up such things as realisation instructions.
- Buy in or design all the necessary tools.
- Contact third-party contractors or suppliers.
- Supervise or instruct those who will be carrying out the actual realisation.
- Draw up the plan of approach; in this case, detail and adjust the overview of the primary activities for each phase in the correct order:
  - a detailed description of the realisation phase, where necessary describing how these activities will be tackled
  - a more general description for the follow-up phase.
- Set up the primary part of the realisation programme.

A number of tips:

- Do your homework.
- In so far as you can judge, ensure that nothing can go wrong.
- Anticipate the possible and allow for the impossible.

Carry out the realisation phase

The realisation phase is aimed at achieving the required project result in one go: the realisation of what was intended, expected and agreed.

Initiative	Definition	Design	Preparation	Realisation	Follow-up
(the idea)	(the what)	(the appearance)	(the groundwork)	(the making)	(the using)

When what has been achieved is what was meant to be achieved

How to achieve this:

- Contract all third parties, works foremen/contractors.
- Carry out the realisation programme.
- Draw up the technical documents for the follow-up phase, detailing the use/operation, keeping and maintenance of the project result.
- Draw up the requirements for transport and installation or reinstallation.
- Train the users, keepers and maintenance personnel.
- Draw up the plan of approach; in this case, detail and adjust the overview of the primary activities in the follow-up phase up to the project result's end of life in the correct order, where necessary describing how these activities will be tackled
- Set up the primary part of the follow-up programme.

A number of tips:

- The project result must be completely finalised at this stage.
- This is what it was all for.
- The use, keeping, maintenance and demolition of the project result must all be in place.

Carry out the follow-up phase

The follow-up phase is concerned with the use, keeping and maintenance of the project result. The whole project finds its ultimate justification in this phase: it must run as planned, goals are pursued and problems diminish.

Initiative	Definition	Design	Preparation	Realisation	Follow-up
(the idea)	(the what)	(the appearance)	(the groundwork)	(the making)	(the using)

The project result must last for the duration of the project

How to achieve this:

– Upkeep the project result.
– Use the project result.
– Maintain the project result and the project tools.
– Improve and modify the project result and the tools.
– Optimise the use, keeping and maintenance of the project result.
– Demolish, destroy or replace the project result.

A number of tips:

– The follow-up phase is the most important phase of all.
– The follow-up phase belongs to the project in the broadest sense, from the unknown start of the initiative phase to the unforeseeable end of the follow-up phase.
– How the follow-up phase will end is not known in many projects.

Specify and arrange requirements

When tracking down and arranging project requirements in the definition phase of a project, it is important to remain thorough, concrete and clear. To achieve this, it is necessary to look for the meaning, significance and origin of the requirements and wishes.

Requirement type	Intention
External interfaces	Requirements that cannot be influenced from within the project and to which the project must unconditionally adhere: conditio sine qua non
Functional requirements	Requirements concerning the performance of the project result: raison d 'être
Operational requirements	Requirements or wishes concerning the application or use of the project result: user oriented
Design constraints	Requirements or wishes concerning the realisation of the project result: 'if it's at all possible, then yes...'

The requirements determine the what of the project

How to achieve this:

- Determine the external interfaces that the project result must meet unconditionally, including the relationship with the relevant environment, by determining what it must link to in the future and what it must take into consideration.
- Specify the functional requirements by indicating what the project result must later achieve, what it must do or cause to be done; which can often be deduced from the goals being pursued or the problems to be solved (look for these requirements by the principal).
- Specify the operational requirements by indicating what the users/clients can, will or must do with the project result; users also include those who must keep and maintain the project result, and the 'users' are also sometimes possible 'victims'.
- Specify the design constraints by finding out what is useful for the makers; remember that by limiting the design in the correct way you avoid 'reinventing the wheel', but doing this too rigorously makes it difficult to reach a balanced project result.

A number of tips:

- A vague requirement is no requirement and an unfeasible requirement does not have to be accepted.
- Requirements must not conflict.
- The external interfaces have the highest priority, followed in descending order by functional requirements, operational requirements and design constraints.

10 **Create constituent projects**

Using constituent projects often makes it easier to retain an overview of the whole project as well as giving an insight into it. Realising constituent projects also demands that all their relevant interfaces or the relationships between them are unambiguously specified, as well as enabling very close monitoring of the interfaces against unauthorised and inadvertent adjustment. Constituent projects offer an opportunity to check the completeness of the project.

Division criteria	Example of a house	Sample document
Object oriented	• The building • The garden • The inventory	• Cover • Page dividers • Pages
Discipline oriented	• Architecture • Electricity Healing installation technique • Landscaping	• Legal • Socio-economic • Financial
Sequence oriented	• Building • Finishing off • Furnishing	• Writing • Printing • Distribution
Activity oriented	• Leisure activities • Hobbies • Household activities	• Reading activities • Decision making activities • Filing activities
Location oriented	• Ground floor • First floor • Attic	• Foreword and introduction • Chapter 1 n • Appendices

The whole is more than the sum of its parts

How to achieve this:

– Split the project up into constituent parts. Constituent projects are groups of activities within a project that logically belong together, taking into account that:
· harmonisation with other parts is relatively simple
· harmonisation within a part is usually based on such things as experience, common sense and knowhow.
– Choose one of the following division criteria:
· the object-oriented line of approach
· the discipline-oriented line of approach
· the sequence-oriented line of approach
· the activity-oriented line of approach
· the location-oriented line of approach
– Specify each constituent project:
· assign the project requirements to the constituent projects
· specify all the interfaces (relations) between the constituent projects.

A number of tips:

– The greater the number of constituent projects, the more relationships there will be to manage.
– The greater the number of constituent projects, the greater the number of activities that can be carried out simultaneously.
– Logically organised constituent projects do not always fit seamlessly into the already existing, permanent organisations participating in the project.

2.2 Manage the project

It is possible, useful and sensible to determine the difference between the primary and the management activities in projects. Failing to do this can often lead to a lack of convenient organisation, a multitude of different opinions and misunderstandings.

Control over a project can be identified as consisting of two main activities that it is not possible to separate: planning and controlling progress.

In a project, there are only five (no more, no less) aspects to manage: time, money, quality, information and organisation. Drawing up plans for each of these management aspects requires the primary characteristics of the project result and of the project itself to be translated into manageable characteristics. As a third ingredient, planning the 'available' resources must be included. If something has to be ready as soon as possible (a demand related to content), that can be translated into: complete by 12 December 2012 (a management demand) by 25 staff members, working for an average of three days a month (the available resources).

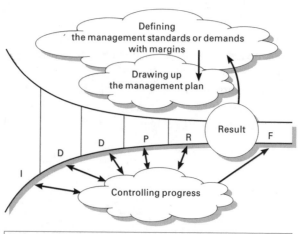

Defining the management standards or demands with margins

Drawing up the management plan

Result

Controlling progress

Rather : making it possible that it **can** and **will** happen
Than   : **doing** the work (primary activities)

In the first place, managing is planning and progress controlling to ensure the correct result

It is true that controlling the progress of each management aspect is mostly done separately, but there are many similarities. The core activity of progress control is a regular and orderly study to determine how far the work in hand threatens to deviate from the plan. Whether or not to intervene then becomes another important management activity.

Increasingly often evaluation is being conducted after the completion of a project in order to learn from what went well and what went wrong. Nevertheless, evaluation can become an activity that is done too late.

Pitfalls:

- There are no clear margins in the management plans.
- The project has to be managed with requirements that are unclear (a broad support base), too wide (optimal), unmanageable (according to the verbal agreement), or too vague (as quickly as possible).
- When controlling the progress of the project, only the history of the project is recorded and the question of whether or not the result will be achieved is not addressed.
- When it looks as if a management plan will be deviated from, the only action taken is to draw up a new management plan.
- As a result of excessive expense claims, the size of the margin incorporated in plans is unknown.

2.2.1 Make the project manageable

No single project can be managed without a great deal of thought and preparation. As manager responsible for the project, you often have to carry out a lot of work to make a project manageable. This all depends on your making unambiguous management plans. Without a management plan, it will be like looking for a needle in a haystack.

Control aspect	Purpose
Time	Ensuring that the project result is realised on time within the margins set and that the project activities are carried out by the (people and means) delegated in the time allotted
Money	Ensuring that the project is profitable within the margins set, that the costs do not exceed budget and that the planned revenues from the project result are (can be) achieved
Quality	Ensuring that the project result is good enough, i.e. that it conforms to the quality standards within the margins set, that interim results are tested against the demands and that the necessary means are available
Information	Ensuring that the project result is unequivocally recorded within the margins set and approved; which of the decision documents is valid, who is party to the information in this document and in which way it may be amended
Organisation	Ensuring that the project result can be handed over and that everyone knows what the tasks, responsibilities and powers within the margins set are of all those involved, as well as what co-operation/and jobs have to be carried out to achieve the project result

It's primarily about controlling the critical (success) factors

How to achieve this:

- Collect management demands, leaving margins for management aspects.
- After intensive consultation with those who are actually going to carry out the work, draw up a clear plan for each management aspect, that has the support of those who helped to draw it up and who are committed to it:
  · the management requirement(s) with margins
  · the management activities that are based on it
  · the necessary resources
  · the relevant progress control.
- Manage/initiate the primary activities in agreement with the management plans.
- Control the progress and then determine:
  · what is still to be done
  · what has already been done
  · are we in accordance with the management plans and, if it looks as if we will not meet these plans or have strayed too far from our goal, what can we do about it?
- Intervene or advise the principal what to do.

A number of tips:

- It is not necessary to manage each requirement concerning content
- One thing to remember about management aspects is: 'a stitch in time saves nine'.
- Managing is not always directing.

Build in margins

Building in margins is essential to the planning of projects. Without margins, no plan or standard is manageable. By using these margins - also the leeway for each management aspect - it is possible to compensate for minor changes without bringing the realisation of the project result into danger or causing it to be delayed. A margin is, then, a translation of an indication of the risks and uncertainties that can be expected in the course of the project.

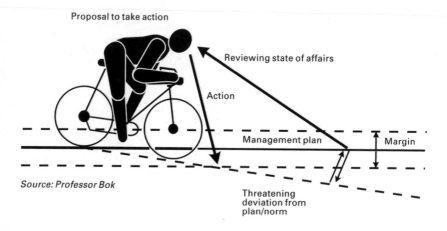

Proposal to take action

Reviewing state of affairs

Action

Management plan

Margin

Source: Professor Bok

Threatening deviation from plan/norm

There must be margins

How to achieve this:

- Determine each management requirement (quantifiable, identifiably present in the project result) and, thus, the upward or downward margin for each management aspect.
- Indicate, where necessary, the margins for interim results or other important milestones for each management requirement.
- Indicate who is authorised to use certain margins.
- Reduce the margins each time a phase is completed.

A number of tips:

- Without margins no one can manage, including the project team member.
- Margins that are too wide are not an encouragement for management.
- Invisible margins lead to exaggeration.

Determine the principles of progress control

It is very important to stick to the management requirements and plans (within the margins) when managing projects. Too often, or too easily, changing these does not promote the credibility of the project manager; nor does stubbornly sticking to an impossible plan.

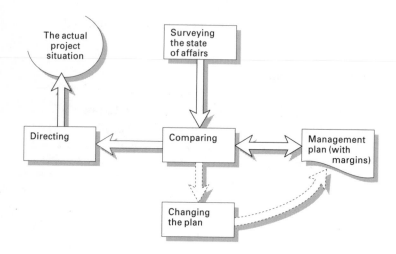

Controlling progress is not post-control but asking: 'Are we going to make it?'

How to achieve this:

- Determine the frequency of the progress control cycle for each aspect.
- Determine the method of progress control (verbal/written, by hand/computer aided).
- Determine the desired data (timeliness, topicality, and aggregation level).
- Determine who delivers what contribution to progress control and when (who compares, who makes the adjustments within and outside of the margins etc.).

A number of tips:

- Controlling progress demands mutual trust and sincerity.
- Controlling progress is, above all, the timely signalling of threatening deviations.
- Nothing can be done about deviations from the plan after the event.

Adjust

Progress control of each management aspect consists of recording the current state of affairs, comparing it with the management plan and making adjustments, or replanning. The aim of progress control is to come up with well-thought-out and feasible alternatives when the threat arises of deviations from plans, in order to ensure that it is still possible to achieve the desired result. In principle, adjusting is ensuring that the plan of approach is carried out in accordance with the management planning.

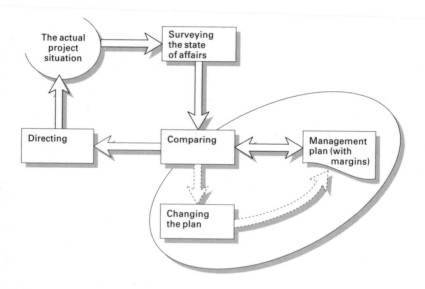

How to achieve this:

- Change nothing unless it proves necessary, for example if the difference between the plan and the actual situation is negligible.
- Make use of the margins to enable work to conform to the management plan, but with fewer margins.
- Make changes to the actual situation that result in the project once more coming into line within the margins of the current management plan when the next assessment is made.
- Have primary activities repeated.
- Shift activities around.
- Look for more diversification.
- Mobilise other capacities.
- Replan, by either expanding the margins or changing the management requirement.
- Develop proposals for adjustments should the project threaten to overstep the margins.
- Advise the principal to stop in cases where it appears pointless to continue the project in its present form.

A number of tips:

- Adjustments that come too late are of no use.
- Adjustments are best applied at the location where the threatened deviation is first observed.
- All management aspects must be taken into consideration before the final adjustment decision is made.

Manage time

With the aid of time management, it is possible to carry out all project activities on time, ensuring that the project result is ready on time and, thus, that the project is achieved on time. Controlling the progress of time means paying attention to ensure that the schedule is kept to. This is impossible without the correct and timely application of capacities and the correct and timely availability of the necessary resources (materials, equipment, space etc.).

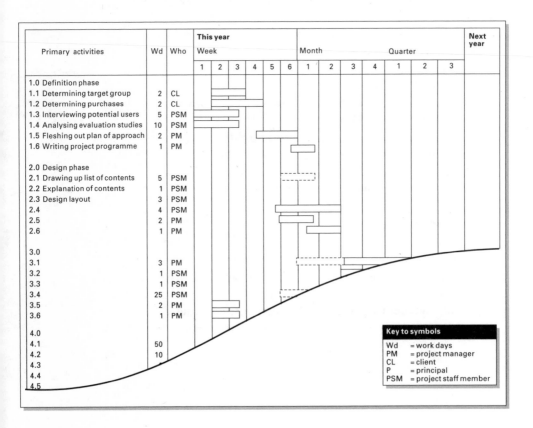

Primary activities	Wd	Who	This year Week						Month				Quarter			Next year
			1	2	3	4	5	6	1	2	3	4	1	2	3	
1.0 Definition phase																
1.1 Determining target group	2	CL														
1.2 Determining purchases	2	CL														
1.3 Interviewing potential users	5	PSM														
1.4 Analysing evaluation studies	10	PSM														
1.5 Fleshing out plan of approach	2	PM														
1.6 Writing project programme	1	PM														
2.0 Design phase																
2.1 Drawing up list of contents	5	PSM														
2.2 Explanation of contents	1	PSM														
2.3 Design layout	3	PSM														
2.4	4	PSM														
2.5	2	PM														
2.6	1	PM														
3.0																
3.1	3	PM														
3.2	1	PSM														
3.3	1	PSM														
3.4	25	PSM														
3.5	2	PM														
3.6	1	PM														
4.0																
4.1	50															
4.2	10															
4.3																
4.4																
4.5																

Key to symbols

Wd	= work days
PM	= project manager
CL	= client
P	= principal
PSM	= project staff member

It must be ready at the agreed time ... and not, therefore, 'as soon as possible'

How to achieve this:

- Determine the desired completion date (with margins) of the project result and of any possible interim results and determine the starting date.
- Deploy the necessary human capacity (qualitative and quantitative, with margins), for each phase and for each primary activity. Indicate if, and if so when and what, materials and/or machines are required. This must always be done in close consultation with those who will later be responsible for carrying out the activities or providing the materials.
- Give details of the turnaround time of each activity to be carried out.
- Relate all primary project activities to be carried out (in sequence and/or parallel) and the necessary capacities to the 'calendar time'.
- Assess/propose the time planning and give your or get a seal of approval.
- Control progress and adjust ... or replan.

A number of tips:

- If the capacity is not available on time, the project result will also be late.
- There is always enough time to do it again, but seldom enough time to conduct good time planning.
- Without margins in time planning, it is not possible to ensure that the project result will be ready on time.

Manage money

With the aid of money management, it is possible to ensure the financially responsible/effective execution of all project activities in order to achieve an economically profitable project.

The controlling of progress in the financial aspects is not only concerned with the effectiveness and legitimacy of the money spent, but much more with the effectiveness and legitimacy of the money still to be spent. After all, nothing much can be done about money that has already been spent.

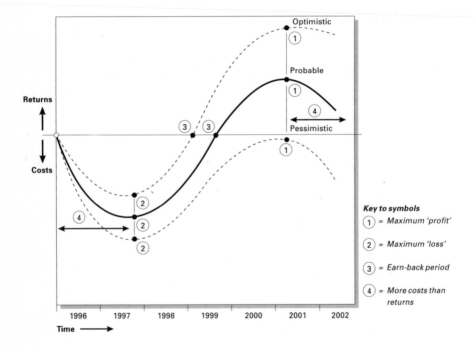

Key to symbols
1 = Maximum 'profit'
2 = Maximum 'loss'
3 = Earn-back period
4 = More costs than returns

**Not: 'Make the project optimal profitable',
but: 'Make it meet the financial requirements'**

How to achieve this:

– Make an inventory of the desired/required/demanded returns (with margins).
– Draw up a cost/benefit analysis, taking internal as well as external points of view into account. Do this in consultation with those who will later bear the responsibility and, where possible, up to the end of the life of the project result.
– Draw up cost frameworks, estimates and a cost budget.
– Allocate budgets(with margins) to constituent projects and to those responsible:
· detailed budgets (with narrow margins) for the imminent phase
· more global budgets (with wider margins) for the subsequent phases.
– Assess/draw up the financial plan and give it your or get a seal of approval.
– Control the progress and adjust ... or replan.

A number of tips:

– Costs that have been incurred do not play a role in the decision whether or not to go ahead: only the interest on the capital invested counts.
– Nothing can be done about budgets that have been exceeded.
– An accurate account of what the project has already cost is not much help to a project manager, certainly when the data in that account is up to three months old.

Manage quality

Quality management helps ensure that all project activities are well executed, in order to attain a satisfactory project result. Trials, tests, assessments and progress control of the quality of the final result of the project are all facets of quality management. Each phase of a project has its own specific quality-progress control activities.

Step	Optimal	User oriented
Primary requirement	Optimal linkage to existing systems	User friendly and easy to operate
Step 1 (Determine which requirements must be controlled/managed)	Does this requirement have to be controlled? If so, then step 2. If not, it is not a critical success factor	Does this requirement have to be monitored? If so, then step 2. If not, it is not a critical success factor
Step 2 (Examine more closely)	What is optimal? Which existing systems?	Who are the users and what are their knowledge and skills? What is friendly? Which of the user-friendly aspects are relevant?
Step 3 (Specify in more detail)	Optimal is (for example): • no repeats in files; each file is, therefore, 'managed' by one system only • no extra conversion by the receiver • no manual intervention Existing systems: • stock-management system (SMS) • financial administration system (FINAS)	Aspects selected are, for example: • ergonomic (resolution of the screen, keyboard, position of the screen) • users manual (top-down structured, written in English)
Step 4 (Make an inventory of specifications)	(Examples) • Which repeats can occur? • Which parties receive which information?	(Examples) • What must be set out in the users manual? • How must this manual be laid out?
Step 5 (Formulate quality requirement)	(Examples) • No repeats concerning: - stock indicators - N.A.C. (name, adress, country) data • No conversion concerning: - production files - prices	(Examples) • All screen layouts must be included in the user manual • The total length of the user manual is approximately n A4-size pages

Not 'it must be as good as possible', but 'good is good enough'

How to achieve this:

- Determine the quality requirements (with margins) for the project result and ensure that these requirements are set.
- Make sure that there are quantified, weighed or demonstrable requirements and point out the quality requirements to contributing parties and to the teams of the constituent projects.
- Indicate when, how and who must report if the quality requirements are being adhered to.
- Assess and lay down the quality plan and give your or get a seal of approval.
- Control progress, adjust ... or replan:
- by, among other things, testing detailed designs and prototypes against the (constituent) project programme, in the design phase; supervising design reviews; designing plans for test tools and test procedures etc.
- during the preparation phase. Making sure, among other things, that the designs are correctly translated into realisation means, instructions and such; designing testing tools and procedures or manufacturing test tools
- by, for example, having tests carried out in the realisation phase; especially entry and process controls and by qualifying as few end controls and adjustments as possible
- by also assessing, among other things, complaints and qualifying renewals in the follow-up phase.

A number of tips:

- Checking, testing, controlling, inspecting and assessing are activities that fall under quality management.
- Self-management is the best management, if you can make adjustments to your own actions.
- Quality is not the 'best practical means' or 'to the best of your ability', because calling to account about quality is only possible if it is calculable, making it possible to enforce. Quality is not what is expected but what has been agreed.

Manage information

With the aid of information management, it is possible to achieve unanimity in the execution of all project activities in order to reach a unambiguous result - one that is able to be reproduced.

It is necessary to ensure that, during progress control of the project information, all parties concerned are familiar with certain 'information bearers': the decision documents. They should contain the most recent specifications of the project result and the primary activities. Furthermore, progress control should be able to provide a continual insight into the status of requests for permission to make changes to these information bearers.

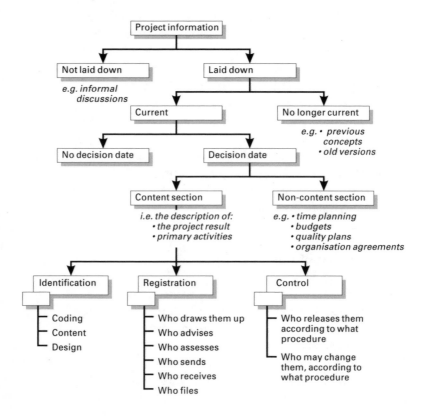

According to the latest verbal agreement, there is no controllable truth

How to achieve this:

– Design an information-management system that contains the decision documents (content description) of this project, the format that is to be used, coding (identification), distribution and filing and ensure that it is accepted.
– Decide who, in this project, must draw up which decision document, approve it, look after or file it and have permission to make changes to it.
– Lay down the approval and change procedure.
– Assess/draw up the information plan and give your or get a seal of approval.
– Control progress, adjust … or replan.
– Register all requests for changes that have been submitted and see to it that a unanimous decision is reached about them which, in turn, is recorded in the relevant decision document.

A number of tips:

– If everyone receives all of the project information, it is not necessary for everyone to learn immediately the matters that are of interest to them.
– That which has been decided on and has been identified as such is true.
– Information management has little to do with communication.

Manage organisation

With the aid of organisation management, it is possible to see that those who are responsible and empowered to do so can and will carry out all primary project activities in order to guarantee that the project result is formally accepted.

The primary task of progress control has to do with the supervision of agreements concerning the division of the actual tasks and the exercise of the powers that these responsibilities entail. Furthermore, the project manager must manage the internal and external communication of the project. Finally, the motivation of those concerned is also a factor that requires the attention of the project manager.

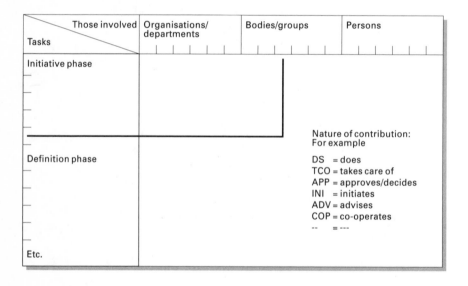

Those involved Tasks	Organisations/ departments	Bodies/groups	Persons
Initiative phase			
Definition phase			Nature of contribution: For example DS = does TCO = takes care of APP = approves/decides INI = initiates ADV = advises COP = co-operates -- = ---
Etc.			

Not 'a client well satisfied with the project result', but 'delivered as agreed'

How to achieve this:

- Indicate for whom the project result is intended, who are the principal, the project manager and those who will carry out the project, the project team.
- Set up a temporary organisation and in it indicate who may decide what.
- Organise the relationships with the players in the environment and, if necessary, draw up a communication plan.
- Put together a project team. Ensure that agreements about co-operation, the functioning of the team, the division of roles, the internal communication and the motivation/effort are in place.
- Design the realisation organisation.
- A project start-up (PSU) is a useful working method to achieve a good project organisation.
- Assess/draw up the organisation plan and give your or get a seal of approval.
- Control progress, adjust ... or replan; for example, consider a change to the composition of the team, the meeting procedure or the way in which conflicts are dealt with.

A number of tips:

- In order to ensure that the project result is put to good use, training is often required for the users, because the use, keeping and maintenance of the project result stop only when that project result is dismantled. And a harmoniously achieved result leads to contented users.
- Co-operation between strangers does not come automatically.
- Bureaucracy and resistance to proposals for action are strong signals that all is not well with the functioning of the team.

2.3 Decide by choosing the correct alternative

The transitions between phases in the course of a project are crucial. These transitions are known as decision points in the project approach. A decision point is a recorded, agreed point of departure - a contract or agreement - that guards against unauthorised changes. Because these decision points are mostly recorded in a document, they are often called decision documents. The decisions taken during transition phases frequently contain a conscious choice among various alternatives. This is reflected in both alternatives for the further detailing of the project result and alternatives for the further plan of approach of the project, as well as alternatives for the management plans.

The complete decision document is normally made up as follows:

- *The project result description*. Depending on the phase in which the decision document is drawn up, this description is more or less concrete. The most detailed description is always to be found in the final decision document: the follow-up programme.
- *The description of all primary activities*. An overview of all the primary activities: in detail for the next phase and more generally for subsequent phases.

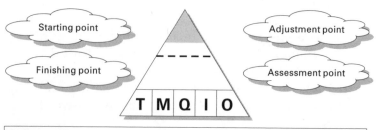

Rather : making a conscious choice at each phase to stop or to continue
Than : carrying on regardless

- *Project management plans*. A management plan for each management aspect:
  · Time management: mentioning the start and finish dates of the project, the completion dates of the various

phases (including margins) and the number of man-hours and other capacities necessary for its completion.

· Money management: the budget, including expenditures and expected returns with margins, where possible worked out for each phase.

· Quality management: quality requirements with margins and the way in which these will be proven or tested in the various phases.

· Information management: the agreements and procedures with margins concerning the way in which the project decision documents are coded, released, distributed, filed ... and changed.

· Organisation management: the project organisation, including the tasks, powers and responsibilities with margins of the principal, the project manager and the project team members. The structure of relationships between the project organisation and the permanent organisation, including committees, steering committees and work groups, and the communication structure both inside and outside the project.

· Progress control: a description of the progress control system: who is responsible for controlling progress, how and how often, and in what way does this person adjust or replan the project or the project plans.

Pitfalls:

– The decision document only contains the description of the desired project result and not the details of its consequences (all the primary activities and management plans).

– There is no decision making at times when this is called for.

– The decision-making process takes such a long time that the project has to be adjusted again.

– A project is made simply to postpone or put off a difficult decision.

– A 'concept decision' is taken just for the sake of having some sort of decision.

1 Ensure that the decision documents are complete

A project is made up of six phases. Because the initiative phase has no start document and the follow-up phase no final document, there is a total of five decision documents.

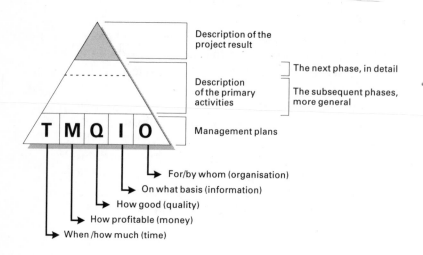

Description of the
project result

The next phase, in detail

Description
of the primary
activities

The subsequent phases,
more general

Management plans

For/by whom (organisation)

On what basis (information)

How good (quality)

How profitable (money)

When /how much (time)

Decision making is choosing among alternatives

How to achieve this:

- Make sure that a decision is complete: which result, which plan of approach and which management plans for T, M, Q, I and O.
- Make sure that the decision is targeted at acceptance and commitment.
- Ensure that the decision can be enforced and is feasible. To this end, you could use the failure factor or risk analysis and incorporate the findings into the margins of the management requirements.
- Make your decisions in order of importance.
- Ensure that each decision is incorporated into a contract of intent.

A number of tips:

- The signature at the bottom of a decision document is not as important as people's understanding of what is going to happen and their willingness and ability to help carry it out.
- A decision document must be unambiguous. If this comes under discussion, change procedures must be started.
- A decision document is never complete, which makes it necessary to have a change procedure.

Construct a project brief

The project brief is the start document for the project.
This marks the formal end of the initiative phase.

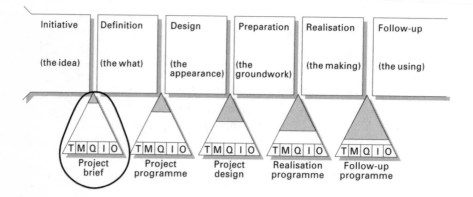

Getting the project brief off to a good start is half the battle

How to achieve this:

- Record the conclusions, agreements and outcomes reached during the initiative phase:
  · the problems or goals that this project must contribute to
  · the desired project result
  · the project's boundaries (what does not belong to it).
- Draw up the plan of approach:
  · in detail for the definition phase
  · more generally for the other phases.
- Grouped per management aspect, record the outcome of the various management activities carried out during the initiative phase:
  · management requirements, with margins
  · management plans
  · agreements for progress control.

A number of tips:

- The project brief has never been fully completed!
- In view of the fact that the project brief contains all the current agreements between the principal and the project manager, it must be understood and supported by all concerned.
- More than 75 per cent of the project can be carried out in accordance with the project brief.

Construct a project programme

Factors applying to the project brief also apply to the project programme.

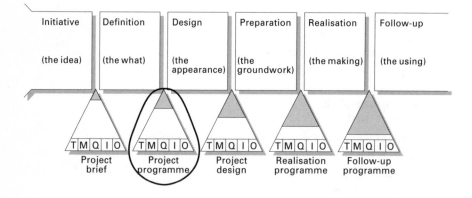

Initiative	Definition	Design	Preparation	Realisation	Follow-up
(the idea)	(the what)	(the appearance)	(the groundwork)	(the making)	(the using)

Project brief · Project programme · Project design · Realisation programme · Follow-up programme

If you have no idea of what has to be achieved, there is no point in carrying on

How to achieve this:

- Record the project result requirements, i.e.:
· external interfaces (external requirements)
· functional requirements (performance, functions and characteristics)
· operational requirements (use, keeping and maintenance)
· design constraints (internal/organisational preferences).
- Record any constituent project.
- Note which demands have been linked to which constituent projects.
- Note the interfaces between the various constituent projects.
- Draw up the plan of approach:
· in detail for the design phase
· more generally for the other phases.
- Grouped per management aspect, record the outcome of the various management activities carried out during the definition phase:
· management requirements, with margins
· management plans
· agreements for progress control.

A number of tips:

- A project programme is never fully completed and must be continually brought up to date by including the latest agreements.
- A project programme that requires continual fundamental change is a bad programme.
- It should be possible to carry out 80 to 85 per cent of the project according to the project programme.

4 **Checklist** **Construct the project design**

The project design originates in much the same way as
the two decision documents mentioned earlier.

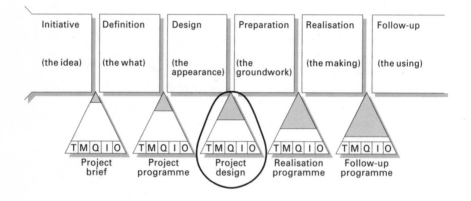

Initiative	Definition	Design	Preparation	Realisation	Follow-up
(the idea)	(the what)	(the appearance)	(the groundwork)	(the making)	(the using)

T M Q I O   T M Q I O   T M Q I O   T M Q I O   T M Q I O

Project brief   Project programme   Project design   Realisation programme   Follow-up programme

Go no further if you do not know what the project result should look like

How to achieve this:

– Draw up the design plans, such as the design drawings, the detailed lists of contents and the layouts:
· for the whole project
· for each constituent project
· in detail.
– Draw up lists for designs and parts.
– Describe the realisation methods (qualitative).
– Describe the realisation tools (quantitative).
– Draw up the plan of approach:
· in detail for the preparation phase
· more generally for subsequent phases.
– Grouped per management aspect, record the outcome of the various management activities carried out during the design phase:
· management requirements, including margins
· management plans
· agreements for progress control.

A number of tips:

– The project design demands a great deal of creativity.
– All materials, tools and aids that play a role in the making, use, keeping, maintenance and demolition of the project result have to be designed.
– The project should now be able to run 95 per cent according to the project design.

2.3.5 Construct the realisation programme

This decision document is built up in a similar way to the first three.

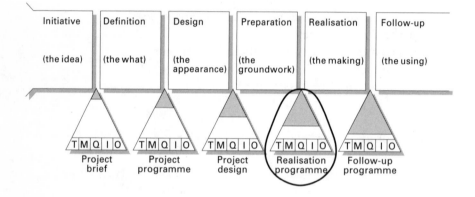

Initiative	Definition	Design	Preparation	Realisation	Follow-up
(the idea)	(the what)	(the appearance)	(the groundwork)	(the making)	(the using)

TMQIO — Project brief
TMQIO — Project programme
TMQIO — Project design
TMQIO — Realisation programme
TMQIO — Follow-up programme

How to achieve this:

- Draw up the result schemes and plans (production and order specifications etc.).
- Make a list of the specified components, such as lists of parts and paragraphs.
- Make a note of the inventory lists of other appliances.
- Describe the realisation methods of production processes (qualitative).
- Describe the realisation tools (quantitative).
- Draw up the purchasing specifications/contracts with third parties.
- Draw up the plan of approach:
- · in detail for the realisation phase
- · more generally for the follow-up phase.
- Grouped per management aspect, record the outcome of the various management activities carried out during the preparation phase:
- · management requirements, with margins
- · management plans
- · agreements concerning progress control.

A number of tips:

- Do not proceed if it is not known what the project result will look like after it has been achieved.
- A realisation programme is never complete.
- 99.5 per cent of everything must be clear by now.

6 Construct the follow-up programme

The final decision document should last as long as the life of the project result.
It is the beginning of the 'endless' follow-up phase.

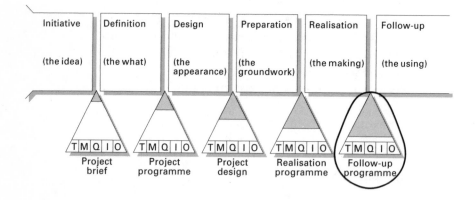

Initiative	Definition	Design	Preparation	Realisation	Follow-up
(the idea)	(the what)	(the appearance)	(the groundwork)	(the making)	(the using)

Project brief · Project programme · Project design · Realisation programme · Follow-up programme

T M Q I O

Is everything completed that must be completed?

How to achieve this:

- Draw up the 'as carried out' plans (revision plans, 'as built' drawings etc.).
- Make the 'as carried out' lists of parts.
- Draw up the detailed plan of approach for the follow-up phase:
- · user manual
- · maintenance and keeping instructions
- · instructions for dismantling etc.
- Grouped by management aspect, record the outcome of the management activities carried out during the realisation phase:
- · management aspects, with margins
- · management plans
- · agreements concerning progress control.

A number of tips:

- Do not proceed unless the complete project result is available, including the completed, endorsed follow-up programme.
- Adjustments made to facilitate use, keeping and maintenance must be recorded and documented; otherwise, in a very short while, no one will have any idea what has been completed.
- Can we learn anything from this project?

2.4 Assess the project

A project manager will want to know, for himself as well as for his principal and other involved or interested parties, how the project is progressing. In many cases, regular progress control of the management aspects will suffice. But in exceptional circumstances, such as in the case of new, unexpected internal or external opportunities or threats, a special assessment will have to be made.

It is also not unusual for one internal or external third party to express a wish for an explicit opinion concerning the project's progress up to the present time, its present state and plans for its future.

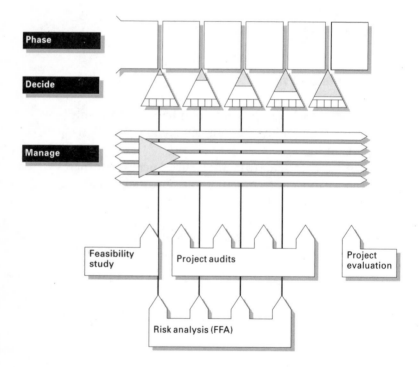

What now?

Pitfalls:

- Despite the fact that they are needed, no replanning measures are in place.
- There is only one form of planning: optimism.
- The role of the players in the relevant environment is unclear: who can help think, who is in the know and who can help decide?
- A project evaluation is carried out for the purpose of finding and punishing scapegoats.
- No one dares take the decision that the result is no longer needed.

Assess the project (at intervals)

Project assessment is usually aimed at pinpointing as many potential bottlenecks or stumbling blocks as possible in a relatively short time. This form of progress control is finely targeted and very structured and requires the co-operation of all those involved.

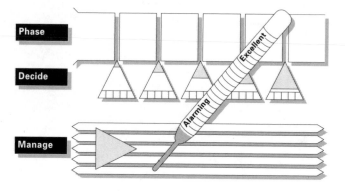

Assessment does not necessarily mean that everything comes to light

How to achieve this:

- Become familiar with the project in question: chart it and its environment by gaining access to the relevant people and documents.
- Gather information from both people and documents: information from the past as well as information concerning the expected future of the project.
- Assess the description of the desired project result in terms of ambiguity and the completeness of the particular project phase.
- Assess the phases that have yet to be carried out for completeness and feasibility.
- Assess the management plans for their attention to detail, use and usefulness, and whether there are sufficient margins in place
- Draw up the project prognosis using well-founded assessments.

A number of tips:

- It is impossible to carry out a good assessment without the co-operation of everyone involved.
- A project assessment is the basis of any possible improvement therapy.
- The assessment process itself can improve the health of a project.

A project audit is a systematic, integral and independent project investigation carried out to determine if a project is being professionally and sensibly approached and managed. It also provides an insight into the possible success of the rest of the project. The result of an audit provides a well-founded assessment and a related set of concrete proposals.

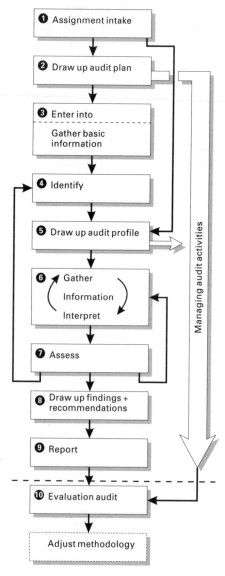

What does an independent third party think of our project?

How to achieve this:

- Determine the contours of the audit: its purpose, depth, aspects and desired outcome.
- Draw up a rough audit plan covering goal/scope, planned stages/approach and those involved/audit organisation.
- Gather together basic information about the project: the latest valid project specifications, primary activities and management plans.
- Identify the project's critical success and failure factors.
- Draw up the audit plan in detail and ensure that conditions and tools are in place.
- Collect, interpret and appraise the necessary project information, from interviews or documents.
- Compile the audit report containing your findings and recommendations, with possible alternatives, and present it.

A number of tips:

- People often feel that a project evaluation also evaluates them.
- The truth about a project is not always the same as an opinion.
- Those evaluated during a project audit must agree to it.

Carry out an occasional project review

A project review is an internal, future-oriented meeting attended by the main players taking part in a project. A review has two aims: to bring everyone up to date with the project's latest developments, and to involve everyone in decision making about the project's future.

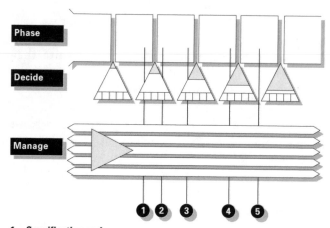

1 = Specification review
2 = Preliminary design review
3 = Final design review
4 = Realisation start review
5 = Transfer review

Reviewing each phase prevents a project's failure

How to achieve this:

- Draw up an agenda for the review meeting (items, sequence, time and participants).
- Come to the meeting well prepared, make it clear what is expected of everyone and point out the open, helping character of the review.
- Ensure that issues are thoroughly aired, that potential bottlenecks are discussed in depth and that everyone is involved in finding solutions.
- During the course of the review, ensure that the interfaces between constituent projects and the relevant environment of the project are respected.
- Ensure that the minutes of the review are clear and precise and that decisions and agreements are phrased unambiguously.
- Ensure that the agreements are carried out correctly according to the normal progress reports.

A number of tips:

- A project review is designed to reiterate the main points of the project.
- A third party who takes on the role of devil's advocate can be very useful in a project review.
- Some principals demand at least one review for each phase of the project.

Evaluate the project

Post-evaluation of a project is only worthwhile if the lessons learned from it are incorporated into new projects. A degree of scepticism is not out of place in view of the fact that every project is unique in terms of such factors as result, commitment, circumstances and environment. However, post-evaluation is to be recommended for people who work intensively together on similar projects.

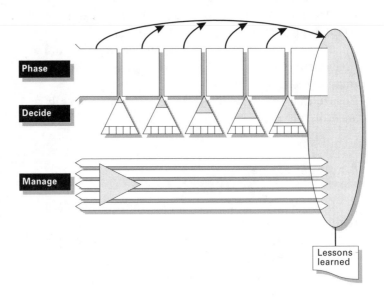

Phase

Decide

Manage

Lessons learned

It is easy to be wise after the event

How to achieve this:

- Make sure that holding a post-evaluation is worthwhile or necessary, that it is not a 'witch hunt', that it is not being held too late in the day, or merely because it is 'always done'.
- Determine the aspects to be investigated, their depth, the approach/method and the sources.
- List and evaluate the collected information and opinions.
- Draw up a list of the 'lessons learned' and distribute it to those who should and those who express a wish to learn from them.
- Organise a 'lessons learned' session and discuss the evaluation and the individual lessons - to be - learned from the projects.

A number of tips:

- People will only learn something if they themselves are motivated to do so.
- Post-evaluation can quickly degenerate into a platform for ventilating annoyance and mutual recrimination. This teaches people little that will help them in a following project.
- Post-project evaluation must be carried out by and with the people who made the project.

3 The programme approach

If a large number of closely linked projects and other efforts or activities have to be carried out within or between organisations, programme management could prove to be useful - for example when an organisation is temporarily engaged in the pursuit of certain goals or when an assignment becomes so complex that it can no longer be overseen. But programme management can also be useful for merging goals that are, in fact, contradictory - for example improved use of a road must be merged with improved road safety.

In addition, programme management can be used in those unique assignments where a large number of relationships between the relevant efforts have to be so closely geared to one another that project-based working is too limited. This situation requires a different, more appropriate management approach to bring this complex unique assignment to a satisfactory conclusion.

Only one thing can be predicted with absolute certainty in programme management: circumstances will change. New parties will want to take part, the 'powers that be' will lose interest or others will do something that make certain activities redundant. Changes will take place both in and around the programme.

Some efforts will be stopped, others will be slowed down and yet others will be initiated. Goals will be adjusted, redefined and added to and certain goals will be dropped.

All these changes can only be managed if the goals being pursued and their relevant efforts have previously been unambiguously recorded. Only then can you be sure exactly how you must react to certain information. You will know, for example, if and how to react to changes in the balance of power. Only then will you be able to judge all the consequences and push through all the proposed and necessary changes relatively quickly.

The programme approach has three main activities: programming, managing and decision making.

Programming is the specification of the goals to be pursued, the agreed efforts designed to achieve them and of the means available. The key activity in programming is carrying out primary efforts.

Managing entails the planning and progress controlling of the management plans based on the goals to be pursued and efforts to be carried out.

Decision making is the final component. This must be unambiguous and integral, and entails preparing decisions, forming opinions and making decisions. The results of programming and managing are integrated in a programme plan. Programme plans for each programme will have to be drawn up at regular, predetermined intervals.

Programming: not just thinking, but doing
In the programme approach, the goals are further defined and, in fact, pursued by programming, i.e. by charting, grouping and carrying out all the possible, necessary, desired and imaginable efforts.

For easy reference, it is usually necessary to bring the various efforts together in a programme structure; this is known as clustering (see Figure 3.1). This clustering can be done in many different ways. Sometimes clusters are made up of the parties involved; sometimes it is easier to categorise the efforts by discipline, source of finance, target group or geographical area.

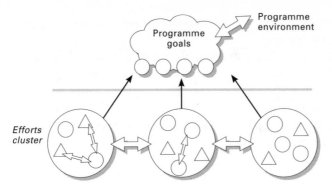

Programme environment

Programme goals

Efforts cluster

3.1   Clustering a programme

In many cases, the goals and the efforts necessary to pursue them can be represented in the form of a diagram, a so-called GEN (**goals/efforts n**etwork). Once completed, a GEN can often be reproduced on a single sheet of A4. This gives it the attraction of being neatly arranged and it is a perfect instrument in communication between all the parties involved in the programme.

A well-compiled GEN can demonstrate which interfaces between the various efforts are considered to be important; for example, by indicating the degree to which any given effort contributes to the pursuit of any given goal. A GEN is set up once and then adjusted, extended or adapted as necessary in a controlled manner. In this way, a GEN forms one of the essential blueprints on which motivated and feasible decisions can be made. Of course, a GEN is also a handy and useful tool that can be employed by the programme manager to illustrate the natural and logical sequence of the efforts that have to be carried out.

Obviously, the whole point of programming is to fulfil the last-mentioned task: actually carrying out all the primary efforts relevant to the programme.

A programme has a life cycle with three stages: start-up, implementation and shutdown (see Figure 3.2). In programmes, the transition from one stage to the next is a more or less natural but always pragmatic moment, when decision-making activities are carried out and when integral and formal decisions are made.

The division between the three stages is marked by programme plans, but these plans can be periodically reviewed during each stage.

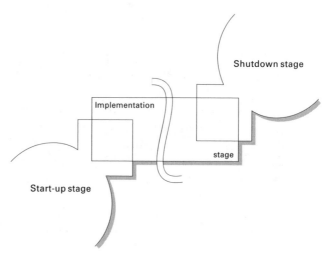

3.2   The stages in a programme life cycle

During the *start-up stage* some of the following questions are addressed:
– Which players (individuals, organisations or parts of organisations) are involved in implementing the programme or can or will become involved with the various efforts? Who will not be involved?
– Which goals do they wish to pursue jointly, and which not?
– Which efforts belong in the programme, and which do not?
– Why have these efforts been integrated into a programme? Why haven't they been tackled routinely or by improvisation, or been integrated into a major project?

The programme grows during the *implementation stage*. The number of projects and other efforts gradually increase, as do the energy and resources being deployed. The programme reaches maturity during this stage.

The *shutdown stage* offers three possibilities: stopping, dividing or transferring.
Stopping entails carefully winding up activities that still have to be carried out. If the programme is divided, the new programmes must be built up at the same time as the original programme is shut down. In this way, it is possible to create one or more new programmes, each with their own life cycle. Transfer means that the programme is effectively shut down. All the programme results and remaining efforts are transferred to the relevant players. Another possibility is to bring all the programme efforts together into a new - permanent - organisational unit.

Managing goal-oriented efforts
Management ensures not only that all the outcomes and interim results from earlier listed and recorded efforts make the required contribution to the programme, but that all the interfaces within the programme and between the programme and its relevant environment are managed and respected. The main points of managing a programme are illustrated in Figure 3.3.

Management is not concerned with carrying out primary efforts but with creating the conditions to make them possible. To this end, management plans must be drawn up that make it possible to control the progress of these primary efforts.

Obviously, the main programme management tasks include more general managerial activities such as inspiring and motivating people and initiating, co-ordinating and ending routine activities within the programme. This often requires the programme manager to take on the role of (delegated) principal for project managers and department heads.

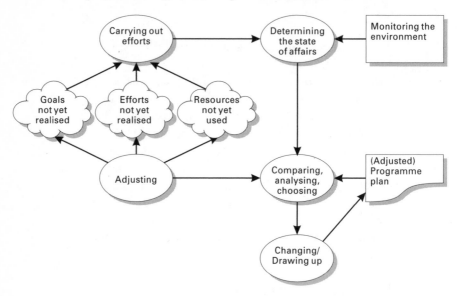

3.3   Planning and progress control in a programme

A programme manager needs criteria in a programme that help him to prioritise and let him compare apples and oranges. In principle, these criteria can be redefined for each new programme. Programme management usually distinguishes five management criteria, making integral management of the programme possible: *tempo, feasibility, efficiency, flexibility* and *goal orientation* (see Figure 3.4). Based on these criteria, the programme manager is able to compare the various efforts and determine if the activities included are the correct ones in view of the goals and the relevant context of the programme.

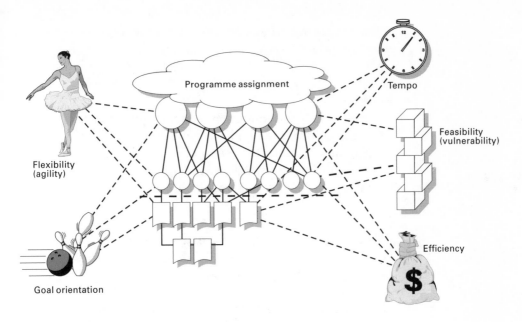

3.4   The management criteria around a programme

These criteria also offer us the opportunity to evaluate and then compare the progress of the programme's various efforts. This information allows us to take a considered and substantiated decision on whether or not to adjust the programme.

The five criteria are defined as follows.

Tempo
This criterion makes it possible to measure and assess the programme's progress, especially at what pace, and when, a programme effort will produce the desired outcome. The earlier any given effort can be completed, the more attractive that effort will be.

Feasibility
Feasibility is a programme management criterion that estimates the degree of possibility of any given effort actually realising the contribution that is expected of it.

Programme activities with the greatest potential for ensuring the pursuing of the goals must be given the highest priority.

Efficiency
The efficiency criterion enables programme management to compare the probable financial value of the programme efforts. The fewer resources necessary for carrying out an effort or the greater its possible return or effect, the more attractive this contribution will be.

Flexibility
Flexibility is the programme management criterion designed to assess the versatility of the effort in question. This flexibility is often demonstrated by the speed with which an effort can be stopped or changed. It also becomes apparent in the way in which capacities and resources can be transferred from one effort to another with the minimum of fuss. Efforts that take up the lion's share of the programme capacities must be carefully managed.

Goal orientation
This criterion allows programme management to measure how far programme efforts can contribute to the stated goals. Of course, highly goal-oriented efforts are preferable.

The value allocated to the various criteria will vary with each programme. In one programme feasibility will be high on the list, while in another flexibility will be considered to be the most valuable. To be able to manage a programme on the basis of these criteria, the value of the criteria in relation to each other will have to be determined. This could be achieved by assigning a particular weighting to each criterion.

Of course, all the criteria within a programme are interlinked. An effort that is very inflexible and that takes a long time, thus scoring badly on the tempo criterion, but that appears to be extremely goal oriented and enjoys wide support could be less lucrative than a very flexible and goal-oriented effort that has narrower support.

If the criteria in a programme are given a specific measure of practicality and a weighting factor, a programme manager will be able to judge each listed effort on the basis of these criteria.

After planning, *progress control* is the second crucial element in programme management. Progress can only be controlled if timely, reliable, complete and, in particular, future-oriented progress signals are being received from those responsible for the various contributions to the programme. All the relevant information coming from the programme's environment also needs to be timely, reliable, complete and future oriented.

Decision making: deciding on goals and all their consequences

The start of a programme is normally invisible and, for this reason, appears simple - but appearances can be deceptive. The start-up stage of a programme - which entails determining the GEM, constructing the programme organisation, searching for and recording management criteria - is anything but easy.

To prevent a programme being carried out blindly, unnecessarily or wrongly, conscious choices have to be made during the life of a project to continue, adjust or stop it. This entails the principal being presented at regularly agreed intervals with plans that require a decision. This frequency is higher during the start-up stage than in the middle of the implementation stage, only to increase again in the shutdown stage.

By taking a decision about the proposed plan, the principal either accepts or rejects what has been achieved up to that time and either agrees to or rejects the programme manager's proposal concerning the efforts for the coming periods.

In this context, however, plan and planning do not only allude to time planning, but also include plans for staff capacity, financial profit and loss, performance and communication.

Figure 3.5 shows a schematic description of the above-mentioned programme approach, where programming, management and decision making are integral components.

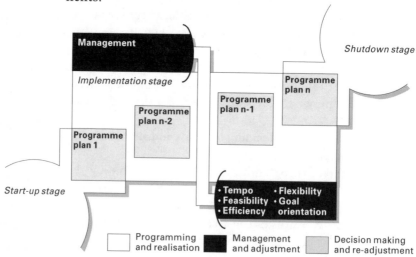

3.5   The programme approach integrates programming, management and decision making

The programme approach really is different

The programme approach is often confused with other management tools. For example, two approaches that on the face of it look similar to the programme approach but are fundamentally different are the open plan procedure and process management. Both these work forms are more a glorified form of improvised working than a management method. The strategic choice approach, strategic management and participatory strategic development are essentially non-managerial approaches that could be used during the start-up stage of a programme; whereas policy programming and planning, for example, is essentially a practical policy-forming method with few managerial aspects or criteria.

These approaches make it clear which primary steps, procedures or activities - in that order - have to be taken, which elements and facets must be taken into consideration and which players and factors play a role. However, in the majority of these approaches the management aspects or criteria and activities are missing. They usually only indicate how the primary activities should or should not be carried out and give no indication of how this work should be managed. Occasionally, these approaches indicate that there are legally binding specific timescales for certain activities, and in other cases the procedural steps are set out or certain players are responsible for them being carried out. But all this has very little to do with professional programme management.

Programme management is not suitable for managers who enjoy freedom from obligation, political opportunism or helpless dependence.

3.1 Specify the programme content

There are normally many people from possibly very different organisations involved in a programme. Frequently these people are all pursuing different, sometimes conflicting, goals.

A programme begins by determining what is being pursued: the goals. As long as these have not been sufficiently clearly specified, carrying out any primary efforts is a risky business. Good goal specification is the basis of a good plan of approach. These goals are determined during the start-up stage of the programme.

Pitfalls:

- It is not clear what does not belong in the programme; the programme boundaries have yet to been determined.
- The target groups, users and 'victims' have not been identified.
- No analysis has been made of the relevant players in the environment.
- The programme has little or no support.
- Only the 'popular' work has been recognised by those taking part in the programme.

Determine the programme goals

The goals justify the programme's existence. The 'ER' goals specify what the programme is pursuing. GreatER turnover, highER profits, lowER costs are examples of ER goals. The goals describe the desired situation.

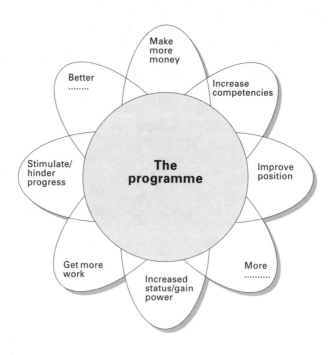

A goal is what those involved wish to pursue

How to achieve this:

- Ensure that those involved consider the programme to be sufficiently important.
- Ensure that all those involved in the programme are aware of their own motives, expectations and opinions.
- Note the relevant problems/bottlenecks in the present situation, or in the near future, and list the possible consequences if the aimed-for contribution to deminish the problem does not materialise.
- Specify the relationship between and the components of the programme's goals (the goal structure); find out all the relevant facts and figures and list the consequences if the goals are not pursued.
- Clearly define the boundaries of the programme's goals, or the problems translated into goals, and state what does not belong within these boundaries.
- Ensure that the programme goals can be and are pursued.

A number of tips:

- Programme goals indicate what must be pursued from any given moment.
- Goals can be described as the pursuit of an ideal: for example, a more profitable turnover from the sale of television sets, less crime in our village or greater efficiency in one of our departments.
- Ultimately, it must be proved that efforts within the programme bring the achievement of programme goals closer.

Programme the programme efforts

Only when a programme's goals have been adequately defined and its boundaries determined can any thought be given to the primary efforts or activities, and the sequence necessary for pursuing them. These efforts are drawn together in a plan of approach. But this must not be overly restrictive: it is only designed to give us an idea of how best the programme can be carried out, taking into account current thinking and present and known future circumstances. For this reason, a plan of approach is always more concrete for tomorrow than for the day after. Insight and circumstances change, as does a plan of approach, but it still has to be managed.

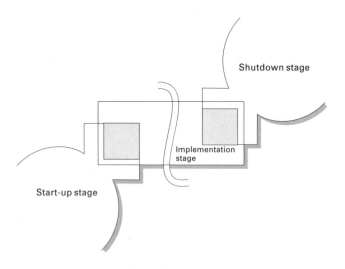

Shutdown stage

Implementation stage

Start-up stage

Programme efforts are described by verbs

How to achieve this:

- Imagine all the efforts that would be worthwhile, necessary or useful to help pursue the goals.
- Imagine this from effort to goal and vice versa.
- Always do this together with those who will be carrying out the effort.
- Determine the natural/logical sequence of these primary efforts and determine which efforts can be carried out at the same time, possibly by splitting them up.
- Make sure that each description of an effort contains a verb.
- State the interim and end result of each effort.
- Specify the tools and material, approach or method to be used for each effort.

A number of tips:

- A plan of approach consists solely of primary efforts, it contains no management activities.
- Clustering can be useful for programmes that contain a large number of efforts.
- The plan of approach contains all the primary efforts within the programme and not only the 'interesting' ones or those from the 'programme organisation' itself.

3 Checklist

Carry out the start-up stage

The start-up stage of a programme is designed for reaching agreement with all the stakeholders and those involved, concerning such matters as the nature, the scale, the importance and the boundaries of the specified programme.

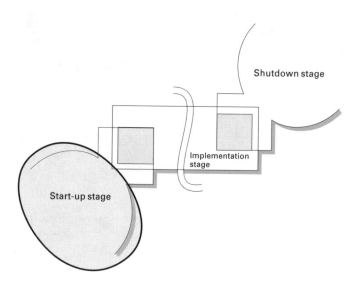

Shutdown stage

Implementation stage

Start-up stage

Look before you leap

How to achieve this:

– Formulate the (subordinate) goals.
– Determine the programme's boundaries, what does not belong in the programme.
– Formulate all the primary efforts aimed at achieving the goals.
– Construct a GEN (goals/efforts network):
· cluster the efforts
· specify the interfaces between the clusters.
– Draw up the primary activities in the programme plan.
– Carry out those activities designated to the start-up stage.

A number of tips:

– The GEN is the cornerstone of the programme.
– ER goals cannot be achieved, only pursued.
– ER goals can be translated into MACIE (Measurable, Acceptable, Committing, Inspiring, Engaging) or SMART (Specific, Measurable, Acceptable, Realisable, Traceable) goals; make sure this is done.

3.1.4 Carry out the implementation stage

The implementation stage is concerned with the actual pursuit of the programme goals by carrying out the planned primary efforts. Another important task is ending the programme in the restricted sense.

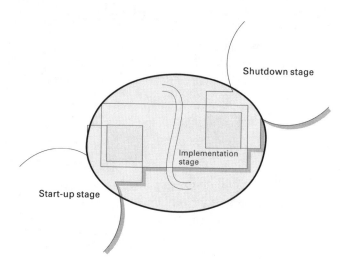

Shutdown stage

Implementation stage

Start-up stage

There will be no effects withour the implementation of outcomes or project results

How to achieve this:

- Carry out the primary efforts.
- Redefine the goals.
- Think up new or additional goals.
- Adjust the part of the programme plan dealing with content.
- Pass on the outcomes of the efforts, including the project results, to those who will use, keep and maintain them.
- Draw up the final programme plan.

A number of tips:

- The implementation stage can last for several years.
- Changes must be carefully controlled, especially during this stage.
- Anything not implemented can be completed during the shutdown stage.

Carry out the shutdown stage

This stage is not part of the programme as such, but it has to be initiated with care. However, this initiation is, in fact, still part of the programme and is concerned with integrating the programme into newly established permanent organisations or existing ones.

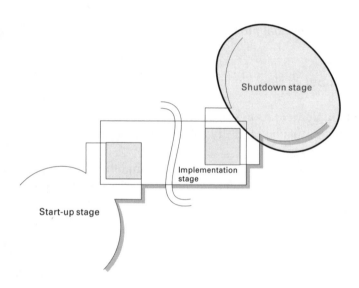

Shutdown stage

Implementation stage

Start-up stage

Even a programme must come to an end

How to achieve this:

- Carry out the primary efforts.
- Pass on the outcomes of these efforts, including the project results.
- Use these results, keep and maintain them.

A number of tips:

- As agreed, the goals must by now have been adequately pursued and the problems must be proportionally less.
- The outcomes of the results of the efforts must now become apparent.
- The programme has ceased to exist, it has been stopped.

The goals/efforts/means network (GEM) of a programme is made up of the goals, the efforts, the means and the interfaces between them. A GEM can consist of a large number of bundled and linked projects or can use subsidiary goals to specify goals via activities and efforts that include a large number of projects.

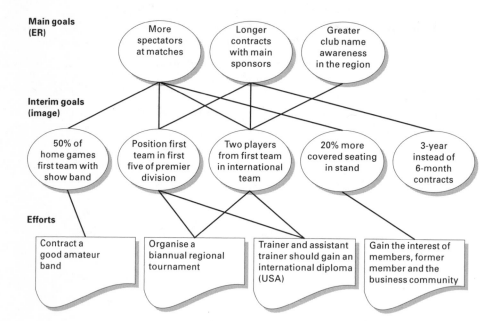

Constructing a GEM is a joint effort

How to achieve this:

– Break down the goals into subsidiary goals.
– Map out the interfaces between the two (a goals network).
– Link the efforts to the goals and state which efforts are expected to contribute to which goals.
– List the priorities of the various goals and efforts.
– Make an inventory of available and necessary means/resources.
– Allocate available resources to the efforts when required.
– Keep the GEM log up to date.
– Make the GEM manageable by discussing it with all those involved and set out the final version.

A number of tips:

– The goals/efforts/means network (GEM) is the cornerstone of every programme.
– Constructing a complete and balanced GEM is not a simple matter.
– The ultimate purpose of a GEM is to gain an overview and insight.

By constructing programme clusters (constituent programmes), it is often possible to maintain a better overview of the whole programme. The clustering also offers insight. However, recognising clusters in a programme demands a completely unambiguous specification of all the relevant interfaces or relationships between the clusters. What is more, vigilance is required to ensure that these interfaces are not changed, either accidentally or by unauthorised persons. Programme clusters offer an opportunity to evaluate the completeness of a programme.

Structuring principal	The most important advantages (+) and disadvantages (-) in black and white
Organisation oriented	+ Easy to delegate - Not cross-departmental
Sequential	+ Justifies the 'natural' sequence - Lead-times are sometimes excessive
Object oriented	+ Promotes goal orientation - Usually difficult to organise
Functional (nature)	+ Makes efficient use of scarce capacity sources possible - Seldom does justice to an inter- or multidisciplinary character
Financial	+ Simplifies the (financial) obligation of responsibility - Is usually illogical
Market oriented	+ Strengthens customer-friendly approach - Does not always prevent duplication
Geographical	+ Makes it possible to use local resources - Can make communication difficult
Mixed	+ All the advantages - All the disadvantages

The whole is more than the sum of its parts

How to achieve this:

- Choose one of the following structural divisions: organisation oriented, sequential, object oriented, functional, financial, market oriented, geographical or mixed.
- Split the programme up into clusters according to the chosen structural category. A cluster is a logically grouped number of efforts and subsidiary goals within a programme where:
· rapport with other groups is relatively simple
· rapport within the group is primarily based on experience and knowhow etc.
- Specify each cluster.
- Link each cluster to the goals being pursued.
- Specify all the interfaces between the clusters, for example outcome and physical relationships.

A number of tips:

- The greater the number of clusters, the greater the number of relationships that have to be maintained.
- The greater the number of clusters, the greater the possibilities for delegation and parallel working.
- The logical division of clusters does not always fit seamlessly into the existing permanent organisations taking part in the programme.

3.2 Manage the programme with TFEFG

Obviously, the primary programme management tasks include more general managerial activities such as inspiring and motivating people and initiating, co-ordinating and ending the routine activities within the programme. This chapter highlights the most important branches of programme management: planning and progress control. These two branches of management are carried out with the help of the management criteria: tempo, feasibility, efficiency, flexibility and goal orientation (TFEFG).

Pitfalls:

- The programme is put on hold for several months during every budget round waiting for authorised financing.
- Although support for the programme has dwindled, it is continued because people are afraid to lose face.
- There are no adjustment measures in place where they are really needed.
- People are happy with qualitative or primary criteria.
- The programme manager has no more powers than a programme co-ordinator.

Put the management criteria into practice

There are five important factors for managing a programme: tempo, feasibility, efficiency, flexibility and goal orientation. Each of these factors must be managed independently as well as in conjunction with the other four.

Tempo is the period of time within which:

- the agreed effects are shown to be present
- the agreed efforts have been carried out
- the agreed capacity (manpower, means and facilities) is available

Feasibility is the probability (degree of familiarity, opportunity) of:

- the agreed effects becoming evident in the future
- the efforts being carried out
- the means becoming useable

Efficiency is the economic desirability of:

- the agreed effects producing sufficient (financial) added value; people being willing to make the necessary sacrifies
- the efforts being carried out
- paying the cost of the use of resources

Flexibility is how far or the ease with which managerial efforts can be delivered, i.e.:

- the agreed effects (to add to, eliminate, increase, decrease) are changed
- the relationship between mutual efforts and between efforts and agreed effects (to add to, eliminate, move) are changed
- efforts and the envisaged effect are realised with the means available (manpower, resources, facilities)

Goal orientation is the degree to:

- the agreed effects make a direct or indirect contribution to the programme goals
- the efforts make a 'measurable' contribution to the agreed effects
- the use of resources, manpower and facilities contributes to efforts and their outcome

---

How to achieve this:

- Get round the table with the most important players.
- Evaluate the value of each effort and programme goal in terms of the management criteria.
- Assign a desired quantitative value to each of the management criteria.
- Based on this valuation, determine the relative value of each effort compared with the management criteria.
- Balance the results until the desired, aimed-for programme of goals, efforts and means is achieved.
- To ensure a broad support base, give all the relevant programme bodies the opportunity to make these decisions.
- Record the outcome and guard it against changes.

A number of tips:

- The management criteria must be made operational for each individual programme.
- A management criterion gives direction to a programme.
- Integral programme management requires focusing on the five management criteria.

Monitor the programme

A programme cannot be viewed in isolation. It is therefore important to monitor the greatest changes to the environment carefully and regularly. This, in turn, usually requires specific instruments such as specifications of effects, measuring instruments and contacts.

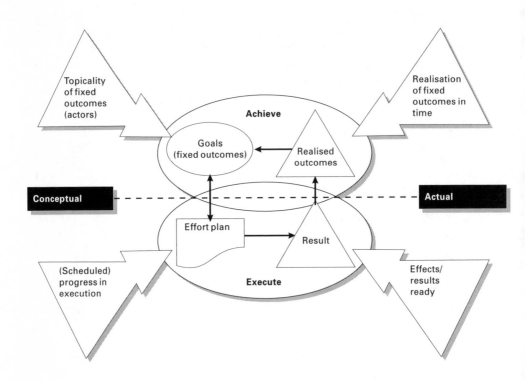

The outside world has a great influence on a programme

How to achieve this:

- Determine what has to be monitored: for example the relevant programme environment, the area to be influenced or the market to be conquered.
- Determine the effects to be monitored and the changes or developments to be observed, such as the growth or lessening of these effects.
- Determine, develop or put in place the measuring method, including the instruments and protocols, together with the persons or bodies charged with carrying it out.
- Turn the monitored information into a proposal for adjusting the GEM.

A number of tips:

- Not all the registered effects are the result of the programme efforts.
- The monitor observes, interprets and proposes adjustments.
- The more turbulent the environment, the greater the need for frequent and careful monitoring.

Prioritise the programme

It is not always possible or wise to carry out all the efforts in a programme simultaneously. Some efforts depend on the results of others, while others are so costly that they have to be postponed. Because the programme environment is so unstable, the priorities of the efforts in a programme will need regular adjustment.

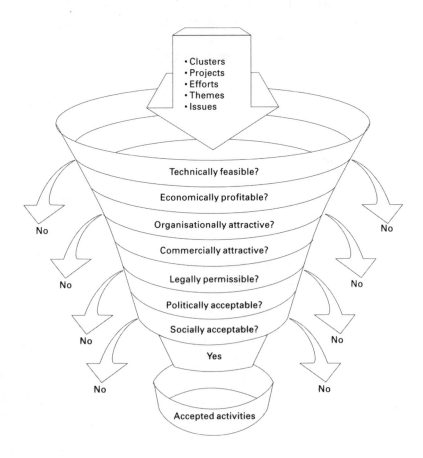

What is important today is usually forgotten tomorrow

How to achieve this:

- Evaluate the comparative value of the management criteria.
- Estimate the contribution of each criterion to the effort.
- Multiply this contribution by the value of the criterion to discover the effort's 'calculated' priority.
- Allow a representative from the relevant players to assess this result: does he agree with it at an emotional, intuitive and instinctive level?
- If necessary, adjust the priorities on the basis of this subjective opinion.
- Agree the circumstances when these priorities should once again be revised.

A number of tips:

- In a rapidly changing environment, the priorities must also be frequently revised.
- Having to change priorities too frequently is a sign of an unmanaged programme.
- It is ultimately the principal who can and must determine the priorities.

Draw up a programme plan

Planning or devising a plan is the first essential step in programme management. This entails drawing up, approving and carrying out programme plans. A programme plan is usually made up of smaller elements, where (constituent) plans drawn up for the immediate future are more detailed, with more definite milestones, more detailed management criteria and smaller margins. Plan or planning in this sense is not restricted to time planning, but also includes the planning of capacities (personnel), finances (profits and losses), performance and communication. As with any plan, a programme plan must address various areas and subjects.

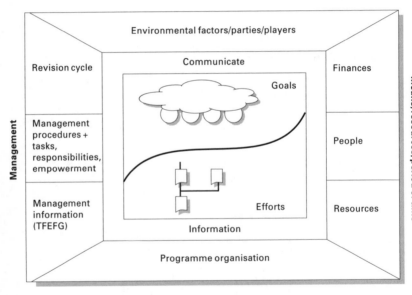

No plan, no progress control

How to achieve this:

- Determine the plan's target group; consider various versions of the plan for different groups.
- Determine the plan's content; consider, for example:
· the goals and the constituent goals
· an overview of the efforts
· the GEM
· the management criteria (including margins) and the management plans
· the programme organisation and communication
· the time planning, including capacities
· the financial plan
· the plans for monitoring and progress control
· the review plan.
- Determine the aim of the plan: compiling reports, verification point, internal communication or communication to third parties, short and to the point or explanatory and informative etc. Then:
· gather together the content
· draw up the plan
· discuss it with the stakeholders, explain it, adjust etc.
· following the agreed procedure, have the final version formally approved by the principal.

A number of tips:

- Working together to draw up a plan makes the plan itself unnecessary.
- Those who draw up a plan for someone else...
- To make it manageable and to be able to control changes to it, a plan must be recorded.

The main players

In the daily stream of activities, the question of who does what hardly arises. People feel free to use their own initiative to deal with matters, or use procedures that were laid down once, in the distant past. In order for a unique assignment to succeed, it is necessary to determine in advance the contribution of all those involved and the organisational positioning of the assignment.

The principal creates the conditions

In normal circumstances, it is clear that management is responsible for initiating and directing activities. Management has, in the past, drawn up procedures and guidelines that enable the staff to carry out the activities with a certain degree of independence. The progress of this work is discussed in the standard management groups, such as management teams and departmental meetings. In the organisation structure, it is laid down who is responsible for what, who manages what etc. But all too often attempts are made to fit unique assignments into these standard procedures and guidelines.

Unique assignments are temporary affairs, which means that it is often all but impossible to fall back on existing structures, procedures, guidelines and standard consultation bodies. Among other things, this means that the principal's function and tasks must be interpreted separately for each assignment. There is often a tendency to attach something unique to one of the organisation's existing management bodies, such as a management team, the computerisation steering committee or the policy board. The motive for this sounds very plausible: 'we meet regularly anyway'. The advantages of using the existing management and other systems must be carefully weighed against the disadvantages. In existing bodies, there will seldom be people who have been selected by reason of their participation in the specific assignment. Therefore, management must look closely into the question of whether it makes sense to have the assignment leader of a unique assignment report to an existing body or whether it is more desirable, for the sake of clarity and involvement, to appoint a separate principal for this unique assignment.

Unique assignments, therefore, demand extra effort from those who are charged with the function of principal. However, it emerges that in daily practice, many managers of all ranks regard unique assignments as being complicated planning issues that have no place in their agendas. This results in them spending insufficient time and energy on fleshing out the role of principal.

The principal is expected to remain involved in the unique assignment for as long as it lasts. At the start he must define the goals and the outcome, ensuring that the necessary resources (personnel, finances and tools) are available. It is possibly even more important that the principal is prepared to assume the role of principal during the course of the assignment, i.e. to direct the unique assignment, by taking decisions on time and making the choices that are necessary for its efficient progress.
He must make it possible for the assignment leader to carry out his work. Furthermore, at set times, he must see to it that the work is adjusted, carried on or stopped. It will be obvious that the principal will and should remain involved for the entire course of the assignment and that it is not only the financial aspect that requires his attention.

When the decision has been taken not to award the job of principal to an existing organisation, the question of whether to award it to a group or an individual arises. Where possible, an individual is preferred. One of the reasons for this is that management unanimity is required. We have learned from experience that frequent consultation is necessary between the principal and the assignment leader, consultation that in many cases cannot wait until the following steering group, committee or management team meeting.

The person eligible for the job of principal is someone who wants the problems solved or who wants to seize the chances offered. This does not necessarily have to be the person who initiated the project or programme - it is someone who will finally be at the receiving end of the project or programme! Put another way, it is someone who accepts the joys and the sorrows of the realisation of the project result or the outcomes of the programme, who can envisage the results of the choices made and who can put the results or the outcomes to good use. A 'good' principal is emotionally committed to the assignment and is willing to take actions and risks. He is someone who does not leave the problem at the office when he leaves for home. Committees and management teams do not remain as committed when their common assignment is in a precarious state. There is a good chance that everyone thinks that one of their colleagues will take the necessary action...

To summarise: a principal is expected to:
- remain involved during the course of the unique assignment
- ensure that the project leader (in his role as delegated principal) is able to carry out the work
- make sure that the decision is taken at pre-arranged times to adjust, continue or stop the assignment
- call the shots, have the last word
- want a problem to be solved or grasp an opportunity
- accept the profits and expenditure from the outcome
- be emotionally involved with the unique assignment and willing to take action and risks
- worry about it.

The assignment leader ensures that the outcome is realised

Each unique assignment needs someone who is prepared to accept responsibility for the realisation of the desired and agreed outcome. This assignment leader, also called the team leader, project leader or programme manager, must be able to exercise the powers that have been delegated to him. These are the powers that enable him to plan all the primary activities and have them carried out in agreement with the plan that has been drawn up. It is important, however, that the assignment leader enjoys supervising a team, coaching people and exercising his power. In order to be able to lead people, he must be capable of focusing his attention on the subject, the behaviour or the problem and not on the person. What is more, he must be able to stimulate self-confidence in his teammates. He needs to be able to anticipate when he himself should take the initiative and when he should give others free rein. Sometimes, consistent behaviour, combined with a positive attitude towards others, is sufficient compensation for a lack of communicative skills and gaps in professional knowledge.

The role of assignment leader is no easy one. He must be able to manoeuvre between professional expertise and managing, between methods and the human factor. In addition to these paradoxes there are others that he has to deal with; he has to operate between a number of extremes (see Figure 4.1).

To a large extent, the tasks, responsibilities and powers of the assignment leader are dependent on the role that he has been given by the principal. It can be the case that a form has been chosen where the necessary resources are not at his disposal and the leader has little or no power over those who are working on the project. This is the case with a 'figurehead' or a 'chairman'. When the assignment leader has executive, operational power over the staff who have been appointed to his project, has his own budget and works with his own quality and information systems, then he can be called a 'manager'.

The assignment leader opts for:		
Formal power	◀ Versus ▶	Informal power
Belief that something can be made	◀ Versus ▶	Belief in natural developments
Autocratic	◀ Versus ▶	Delegation
Independent ego	◀ Versus ▶	Serving ego
Patience	◀ Versus ▶	Impatience
Supportive	◀ Versus ▶	Steering
Rigid	◀ Versus ▶	Flexible
Manager	◀ Versus ▶	Leader
Counting facts	◀ Versus ▶	Counting feelings
Concrete	◀ Versus ▶	Abstract
Perfection	◀ Versus ▶	Ambiguity
Main lines	◀ Versus ▶	Detail
Action-focused	◀ Versus ▶	Reflective
Complex	◀ Versus ▶	Simple
Today	◀ Versus ▶	Future
Verbal	◀ Versus ▶	Written
Good method	◀ Versus ▶	Good person

4.1   The assignment leader makes his choice

Whatever title the assignment leader has, it is always his task to initiate the primary activities.

In order to avoid working at cross-purposes - and at cross-purposes with the principal - he must also ensure co-ordination between the various parties involved. One of the assignment leader's main tasks is to ensure that there are management plans in place, with the necessary margins, to make the progress controlling of the unique assignment possible. Sometimes he draws these plans up himself; sometimes this is done by the line manager. In the latter case, the assignment leader must ensure that it is clear who is responsible for controlling the progress of the plans and what method is used. If everything is clear one task remains, namely controlling the progress of these plans or seeing to it that someone else does this. For example, in a small project, the assignment leader draws up his own time schedule and budgets. In a larger programme, he has assistants to do this.

The assignment leader is expected to be someone who likes and gets on with people. He must be willing and able to influence other people - team members, bosses, interested parties and others in his environment. For this, it is necessary for him to exercise his powers and be able to communicate with people. It is essential that the attitude of an assignment leader is result oriented. Unlike the line organisation, where the activities are directed towards continuity, in a unique assignment everything is directed towards a previously determined outcome. It is vital that the assignment leader believes in the outcome, otherwise it will be obvious that he is merely going through the motions. He must be emotionally involved with the work in which he is engaged: he must think that there is a point to it and that it can be realised.

He must also enjoy working with other people, because, after all, such a thing as a programme is not a one-man show but a temporary co-operation between people who originate from various disciplines, and often even different organisations; it is the assignment leader who binds the whole together.

The assignment leader must not only be a good judge of character, he must also be familiar with the organisation in which the unique assignment, for the most part, takes place. For example, he must have an insight into the formal division of tasks, responsibilities and powers in order to make the best use of them for his assignment. It is only then that he can judge when something must go through the formal channels or when it can be dealt with informally.

An assignment leader must be capable of explaining, beforehand, to his staff and to the principal just how he intends tackling the unique assignment. If those involved are aware of the approach that is being used, they will know what has to be done when and when they must have an answer to which questions.

In small projects, the assignment leader will do most of the primary work himself. Such situations demand that his knowledge is primarily professional and that he is adequately skilled in the supervision of personnel. In some cases, it is sufficient for him only to be conversant with the terminology of the various disciplines, enabling him to assess contributions at project as well as at programme level.

In a unique assignment, the tasks of the assignment leader are often rather vague, and as far as determining his authority, the situation is not much better. If an assignment leader is to justify the responsibilities with which he has been entrusted, he needs to be empowered to assign work to his team members, within the framework of the agreed plan. What is more, he must at least have the power to take corrective measures within the margins of the management plans and the relevant agreements.

To summarise: an assignment leader is expected to:
– compose the description of the intended project result or of the goals of the programme being pursued
– draw up the relevant plan of approach
– initiate the primary activities
– act as co-ordinator for the various parties involved
– draw up management plans for the programme or project
– ensure that these plans contain adequate margins
– make clear who controls the progress of these plans and the way in which it is done

- ensure that the plans are adjusted
- be aware that part of his task is to keep an eye on the internal relationships within his unique project
- influence the environment and anticipate changes in external factors relevant to the assignment.

The assignment team member does the work

A team is a team only when its members can and want to feel co-responsibility for the realisation of the project result or for pursuing the goals of the programme and for each other's contributions. In Chapter 6, the characteristics and functioning of teams are dealt with in more detail. The results of the individual efforts can add up to more than the sum of the whole. The assignment leader plays a guiding role only when it proves necessary. Assignment team members are given, and take advantage of, sufficient latitude to enable them to confer with each other and decisions are taken for each individual situation. Sometimes it is the specialist who takes the decision, sometimes there is a majority vote and sometimes the assignment leader himself takes the decision.

No matter how the team is organised, it is always the task of the team member to use his expertise to carry out activities within the bounds of the previously drawn-up plans and to report, whether requested to or not, to the (section) assignment leader.

Besides their professional competence, the main thing that distinguishes effective and competent assignment team members from ineffective ones is their enthusiasm, social intelligence and involvement in the realisation of the unique assignment. They can give meaning to the first rule of a team worker: latitude is the product of self-management, taking the initiative and knowing when to ask for assistance from colleagues or from the assignment leader. Well-functioning staff will appreciate it if they are delegated tasks and responsibilities, and given the authority that corresponds to their level of competence. They will have to learn to live with the 'worker's paradox': in principle, they should feel as if they are the assignment leader's equal; but, at the same time, they must recognise the differences regarding operational tasks, responsibilities and empowerment.

Another characteristic of being a team member is that they are not only involved with their own goals and ambitions but also with those of the unique assignment. Irrespective of the nature of the assignment, it is important for assignment team members to commit themselves fully to the task that the team has to tackle. Furthermore, they must have good communication skills and be able to share responsibilities and power with others. The readiness to accept help and to help others is important. In order to bring a unique assignment to a successful conclusion, team members must be capable of working within a relatively informal framework.

There are not many assignment team members who like to be told this, but in order to be able to function well in a team working on a unique assignment, you must have a certain amount of skill in reading plans and be prepared to work, often for long hours, with (limited) previously determined resources.

The practice of unique assignments has positively demonstrated that working with more than one boss is often a real necessity. The attitude of the team member is not entirely determined by himself. In part it is determined by the ideas and behaviour of the assignment leader, and by the organisation in which he usually works. There are probably few assignment team members who do not spend part of their time working in a permanent organisation - the organisation (the section, group or department) that is their home base. Here, their operational boss decides what they do, while their functional boss decides how and by which method or means. In the permanent organisation, the functional boss will also bear the responsibility for furthering expertise and, in his function as (hierarchical) boss or chief, for monitoring the personal well-being of the worker: holidays, rewards and co-ordination of assessment reviews.

It is essential that people who work on unique assignments are able to function if these three bosses are not united in one person. This means that a person may be accountable to project leader A for the operational activities in one unique assignment, for another to programme manager B, while, at the same time, the organisation structure requires him to report hierarchical to his own department chief on both assignments. To complicate matters further, he could also be receiving functional support from an external consultant for project A, while being given support by a colleague from another department for programme B.

To summarise: an assignment team member is expected to:
– contribute his expertise
– carry out the agreed activities in the previously determined plans and report progress to the (section) assignment leader, whether requested to or not
– know how to cope with the 'employee's paradox': to consider himself the assignment leader's equal while, at the same time, recognising the difference in their tasks, responsibilities and powers.
– be capable of communicating and sharing power and responsibility with others
– be willing to both give and receive help from others
– be able to work in conditions where the structure and balance of power are more relaxed
– be able to work with more than one boss at any one time.

Organising the workers

The tasks, responsibilities and powers involved in assignment leadership can be delegated to those involved in many different ways. Everything can be delegated to the management of the permanent organisation, whereby a 'dependent organisation' is created for the unique assignment. On the other hand, it is possible to delegate everything to the management of the unique assignment, the assignment leader, with an 'independent organisation' for the unique assignment. The many variations in between delegate some tasks with the relevant powers and responsibilities to the management of the permanent organisation, and the rest to the assignment leader (see Figure 4.2). Just as there is no general concept for the structuring of organisations, neither is there anything cunclusive laid down for formalising the relationship between a permanent organisation and the organisation that is to realise the unique assignment.

Various forms or structures can be distinguished in the dependent organisation, including the co-ordination structure and the consultation structure. In the co-ordination structure, the organisation of the unique assignment consists of little more than a part-time assignment leader and employees who contribute towards the assignment from within their own organisation. The assignment leader has little or no operational authority over the people who are involved in the execution of the assignment; this authority remains in the hands of the management of the units of the permanent organisation or organisations. The assignment leader merely follows the progress of those involved and keeps them informed of the state of affairs with others. Only the management of the permanent organisation or the principal is able to steer/adjust, because the formal authority given to the assignment leader is inadequate.

There are two main variants of the consultation structure: one in which the bosses carry out the consulta-
tions and one in which those involved consult with one
another. For some unique assignments, a team is
appointed that consists of chiefs who make no other
contribution to the assignment than the collection and
delegation of work for their employees. In the second
main variant, the team leader calls those involved
together for a meeting to discuss progress and, if this is
permitted, to make agreements about possible future
activities. Whichever dependent organisation for the
unique assignment is chosen, the main influence of
the permanent organisation remains there, often to the
cost of the unique assignment.

In an independent organisation set up for a unique
assignment, the assignment leader is allocated his
own sources of capacity. In some structure variants of
the independent organisation, the assignment leader
and the team have all the powers necessary to bring the
unique assignment to a successful conclusion. Sometimes employees are appointed to the team for a fixed
number of days, they have access to their own financial
resources and they can work with their own quality
and information management systems.

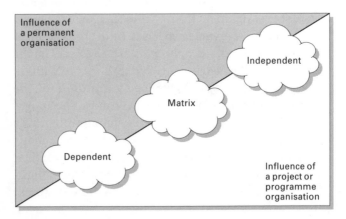

4.2   Various organisational forms for unique assignments within a
permanent organisation

Which variant is most suitable for which situation? The dependent variants are the most suitable if what is most important is that the permanent organisation accepts the outcome of the unique assignment and it is not interested in managing it directly. Matters such as costs are, in these variants, difficult to trace back to the assignment, since they remain within the accounting of the individual departments. This means that the assignment leader has no influence over the costs; the department bosses decide on expenditure. Even though the assignment leader has little operational control, his informal influence can nevertheless be considerable if he is well versed in the ways of the department and is fully accepted by those involved. In the dependent structure variants, an important task for the assignment leader is, then, to maintain relations with and between departments in the organisations that are contributing to the assignment. In view of the fact that much is done informally, in order to cultivate goodwill the assignment leader must regularly draw the attention of those involved to the fact that they are dealing with a team engaged on a specific assignment.

The independent structure variants are particularly suitable for important assignments and where the outcome is the prime consideration. The costs involved are apparent and the assignment members are accountable, since they control all the resources for achieving a successful assignment.

4.1 Recognise organisational differences

The permanent organisation and the organisation for the unique assignment are interwoven, but they both have their own specific characteristics with regard to structure, personnel, management style, systems, culture and strategy.

Obviously, there will be differences between the two organisational forms. This becomes manifest in the form of unavoidable and natural tensions between them.

Permanent organisation		Organisation of this unique assigment
• Vertical Hierarchical Changable	Structure	• Horizontal Co-ordinated Streamlined
• Activity oriented Enterprising	Personnel/ management style	• Result oriented Concluding
• Year planning Departmental budgets It could be better	Systems	• Project planning Consituent project budgets Good is good enough
• Avoid precedents Routine Club spirit	Culture	• Adhoc reactions Situational Team spirit
• Continuity	Strategy	• Temporary

Tension
• Unavoidable
• Natural

Differences manifest themselves in tension

How to achieve this:

- Find out what the real differences are.
- Deal with these differences by:
  · compensating for them
  · ignoring them
  · changing them.
- Gear the organisation of the unique assignment to the possibilities of the permanent organisation on the one hand, and the interests of the assignment on the other.
- Record any findings, for a project in the organisation management plan of the relevant decision document and for a programme in the programme plan.

A number of tips:

- Learn for the future from the tensions of today.
- Avoid duplication of procedures.
- Flexibility is a key competence for people working in unique assignments as well as in permanent organisations.

Determine the desired organisational form

It is important to gear the organisation for a unique assignment to that of the permanent organisation, paying particular attention to the division of influence between both organisations.

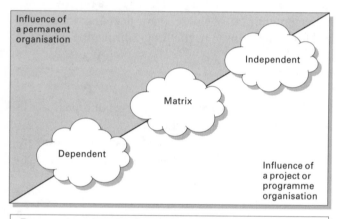

Influence of a permanent organisation

Independent

Matrix

Dependent

Influence of a project or programme organisation

• Types must vary in each unique assigment
• Types can vary in each phase/stage

There are an endless number of organisational forms for unique assignments

How to achieve this:

- Determine who has an interest in the unique assignment and the nature (size, direction and scope) of their interest.
- Acquaint the principal with his tasks, responsibilities and powers.
- Appoint an assignment leader and advise him of his tasks, responsibilities and powers.
- Appoint the assignment team members and advise them of their tasks, responsibilities and powers.
- Make clear agreements with interested parties.
- Record information in the relevant decision document from the project's organisation management plan or in the programme's programme plan.

A number of tips:

- Wait for the 'not invented here' effect.
- A vitally important unique assignment is easily accepted and offers a great deal of scope.
- An organisation for a unique assignment is by definition changeable, but controlled.

Fill three key positions

There are three key roles or main players in every unique assignment: the principal, the assignment leader and the assignment team member. The assignment team member enjoys his work and does what he has to do. The assignment leader is closely involved and wants to justify his role in the assignment. The principal has the motivation, mentality and resources, and wants a result and/or outcome.

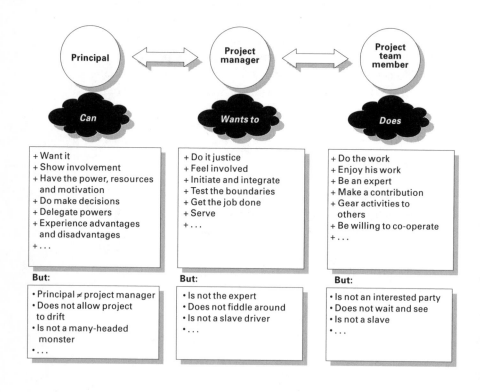

Principal ⟷ **Project manager** ⟷ **Project team member**

Can — *Wants to* — *Does*

+ Want it + Show involvement + Have the power, resources and motivation + Do make decisions + Delegate powers + Experience advantages and disadvantages + . . .	+ Do it justice + Feel involved + Initiate and integrate + Test the boundaries + Get the job done + Serve + . . .	+ Do the work + Enjoy his work + Be an expert + Make a contribution + Gear activities to others + Be willing to co-operate + . . .

But: / **But:** / **But:**

• Principal ≠ project manager • Does not allow project to drift • Is not a many-headed monster • . . .	• Is not the expert • Does not fiddle around • Is not a slave driver • . . .	• Is not an interested party • Does not wait and see • Is not a slave • . . .

The formal organisation of the unique assignment must also be right

How to achieve this:

- Look for the right principal:
  · find out what he wants
  · judge his intrinsic involvement
  · verify to what extent he can deliver what is necessary for this unique assignment.
- Select the right assignment leader:
  · assess his competence
  · check that he is sufficiently independent
  · ensure that he is up to the task.
- Appoint the right assignment team members:
  · assess their competence
  · assess their willingness and availability
  · ensure that there is a good climate of co-operation.

A number of tips:

- Make sure that the principal is not a many-headed monster.
- The assignment leader does not have to be the expert.
- The assignment team members must not promote the interests of their 'departments'.

4.4 Fill the role of principal

Before a unique assignment, project or programme can formally begin, it must be clear who the principal is. This is a crucial decision. More unique assignments go wrong for the lack of, or the wrong choice of, a principal than for any other reason. The (delegated) principal is the person in the organisation who can and does ensure that the conditions are in place to allow the unique assignment to succeed.

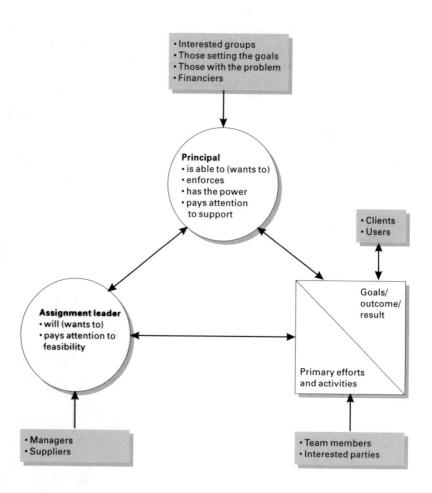

**A good principal can and does ensure that the
unique assignment is carried out**

How to achieve this:

- Make it clear to everyone that you really expect the unique assignment to be carried out: that you expect a project result and/or programme outcome.
- Ensure that you are in sole charge of the unique assignment, that you have the last word.
- Stay involved and let everyone see this.
- Ensure that the assignment leader has the resources to carry out his work and do not get under his feet.
- At the request of the assignment leader or on your own initiative, decide whether to adjust, to continue or stop the assignment, or delegate this choice.
- Accept the profits and losses.
- Become emotionally involved with the unique assignment and be prepared to take risks.
- Let it keep you awake.

A number of tips:

- The principal ensures continued support.
- The principal provides resources.
- The principal chooses a good assignment leader.

4.5 Fill the role of assignment leader

The leadership of almost every unique assignment is similar, in as much as the assignment leader shares responsibilities and powers with others outside the unique assignment who do not necessarily have a more senior position in the parent organisation. Another characteristic of unique assignments is that its leadership is often shared by a number of people. Thirdly, the people carrying out the unique assignment often have far more professional knowledge of it than the person leading it.

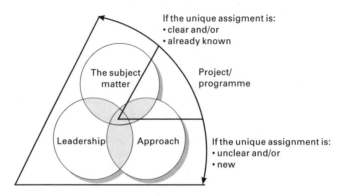

If the unique assigment is:
- clear and/or
- already known

Project/programme

The subject matter

Leadership   Approach

If the unique assignment is:
- unclear and/or
- new

An assignment leader is not a jack-of-all-trades

How to achieve this:

- As an assignment leader, be goal and/or result oriented, tenacious, ambitious and independent.
- Where necessary, free the assignment from restrictive and obstructive procedures.
- Keep your competencies up to date:
- leadership (managing and supporting)
- the subject matter (not too one-sided, be aware of the patterns)
- the approach
- When appointing an assignment leader, ensure that he has all the necessary competencies:
- knowledge (does he know enough, is his knowledge multifaceted?)
- experience and expertise (can he do enough, does he have proven capabilities?)
- attitude (does he want it enough, is he sufficiently motivated?)

A number of tips:

- You cannot become a professional assignment leader overnight.
- Never wrong-foot your principal.
- Give your assignment team sufficient scope.

Fill the role of assignment team member

Only when those charged with carrying out the unique assignment feel a measure of joint responsibility for it and for each other's contribution to it can there be any talk of an assignment team. The results of all the activities or efforts are then greater than the sum of the individual activities or efforts. The team member is the powerhouse of every unique assignment; after all, he is the one who has to carry out the primary tasks.

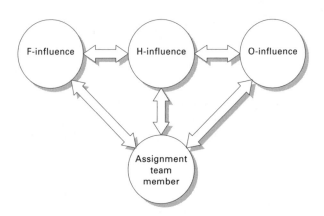

Functional	Hierarchical	Operational
• How • Which approach • What tools • Which methods • Development of expertise • Who	• Personal well-being • Personal development • Remuneration, holidays etc. • Assessment co-ordination	• What • When • Which budget • How good • On the basis of... • Together with...

No unique assignment would ever be completed without the aid of motivated team members

How to achieve this:

- Bring in the necessary expertise.
- Carry out the agreed activities within the previously determined plans.
- Whether requested to or not, report progress to the assignment leader.
- Recognise the 'assignment team member's paradox': regard yourself as the assignment leader's equal, at the same time recognising the differences in such matters as operational tasks, responsibilities and powers.
- Communicate with others, in order to share responsibilities and powers.
- Help others and let them help you.
- Work without overly rigid structures and power balances.
- Be willing to work for more than one boss at the same time.

A number of tips:

- If you don't do it perhaps no one else will, but it has to be done.
- It's not about doing your best, but about doing what has been agreed.
- In a unique assignment, the person who knows is not always permitted to say.
- Waiting until something is noticed is an extremely serious transgression in a unique assignment.

4.7 Checklist

Determine your style of leadership

Leadership entails influencing the performance of others through personal contact. It uses words such as organise, motivate, instruct and delegate. The best style of leadership is geared to those whom you are supervising and the work that they are carrying out. Employees usually enjoy working independently and this increases motivation, giving the manager more scope to deal with other matters.

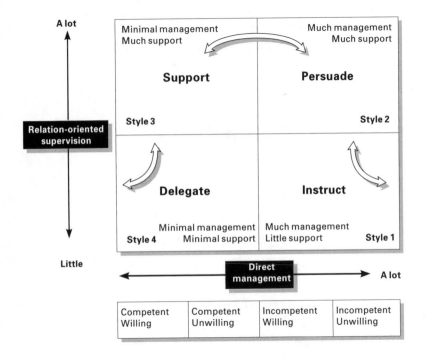

| Competent Willing | Competent Unwilling | Incompetent Willing | Incompetent Unwilling |

'What's sauce for the goose is sauce for the gander' is not true in unique assignments

How to achieve this:

- Instruct if the team member is less competent and unwilling. Give precise written instructions and carefully control their implementation.
- Persuade if the team member is less competent and not very willing. Offer clear guidance and give emotional support if necessary.
- Support if the team member is competent but not very willing. Offer little guidance, but forcefully motivate.
- Delegate if the team member is competent as well as willing. Delegate as much work as you can, create the right conditions.

A number of tips:

- Encourage your team members to take their job seriously.
- Gradually reduce the amount of supervision and accept the increased risk.
- Be quick to offer positive feedback when performance improves.

4.8 Checklist As an assignment leader, acquire sufficient power

Power can be understood to mean being able to influence or direct other people's behaviour to a certain degree.

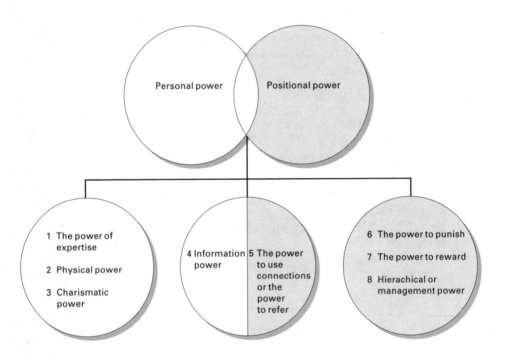

Personal power

Positional power

1 The power of expertise

2 Physical power

3 Charismatic power

4 Information power

5 The power to use connections or the power to refer

6 The power to punish

7 The power to reward

8 Hierachical or management power

The authority you get from the shopfloor is more important than the power that goes with the job

How to achieve this:

- Make sure that you have a voice in determining resources (jobs, money, tools etc.).
- Gather information about relevant processes, products and services.
- Get to know important people/bodies (obligation/reputation).
- Ensure that people want to identify with you personally or with your ideas.
- Ensure that other people believe that they depend on you.

A number of tips:

- Fear is the motive for not doing something.
- Someone who checks everything sees nothing.
- Showing trust engenders trust.

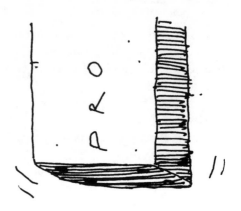

Environmental factors and players

Each unique assignment must take into account the environment in which it operates or in which its outcomes have to be integrated. Important factors include the physical environment of a project result, where it will be in place, how it interfaces with other objects already there and the delivery and transport channels. The technology to be used and the financial means can also be important factors. However, most factors can be influenced by the players, which is why this chapter is primarily concerned with them. In a unique assignment many different players can be involved. (See figure 5.1)

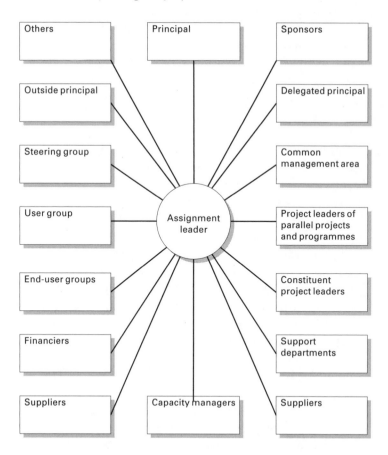

5.1   Many players are involved in unique assignments

Those most directly involved - the principal, the assignment leader and the assignment team members - were discussed at length in Chapter 4. Here we deal with those who are less directly involved, which does not always mean less important. On the contrary, the players in the relevant environment often have a decisive role in the success or failure of a project or programme, even if only because they are the ones who must apply or use the result or outcomes, or because a unique assignment needs external financing.

Players are parties or people who can and do exercise their influence from within the relevant environment of a project or programme. This influence can be so far-reaching that it forms part of the boundary conditions, e.g. legislative. Less far-reaching influence are possible in the form of co-financing, supplying, passive tolerance and so on. Other terms that can be used in this connection are support, context, terrain and field.

Everyone and everything that does not belong directly to the project or programme forms part of its environment. Everyone and everything that can or will influence the project or programme is part of the relevant environment. No matter how good the planning of a unique assignment is, or how enthusiastic and professional the approach, the relevant environment continually can throw a spanner in the works. People withdraw their support, they want more involvement, they suddenly want something different. The principal and the assignment leader bear the primary responsibility for influencing these environment factors and continually regulating them.

Figure 5.2 illustrates which internal and external players can be involved in a unique assignment. Four segments are distinguished in which those involved can be situated. However, it is not always clear beforehand if a certain player will operate internally or externally.

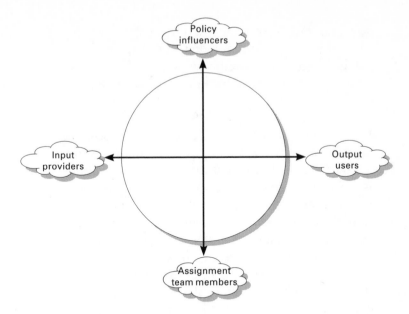

Four categories of external players

External influencers

Those influencing policy, ultimately in the person of the principal, have an influence on the reason for the unique assignment. This means that they help to determine the desired outcome - the 'what' - of the unique assignment. There are three categories of people who can influence policy: financiers, sponsors and those representing various interests.

If access to financial resources is important - and when is this not the case in unique assignments? - financiers are important. After all, they provide the necessary resources. Furthermore, these resources can be used for different purposes, because money is easily converted into other things such as raw materials, equipment and manpower.

Sponsors are especially important for unique assignments that are, to a degree, controversial. They are the people who can ensure that, where possible, the project or programme receives positive treatment. In all bodies where they are active, they radiate their support for the unique assignment. Whether requested to or not, they defend the initiative whenever and wherever they think fit.

Those representing the interested parties form the third, however not very homogenous, group of influencing factors. Their attitude towards the unique assignment cannot be simply described as being positive or negative. Some will exercise all their influence to thwart the unique assignment, while others will do their best to ensure that it succeeds. Neither the representatives of interested parties nor their intentions are always recognisable at the start of a unique assignment. They can suddenly appear on the scene, such as an action group that is formed with a specific goal in mind, or spontaneous protest groups.

Input providers
Input providers are the parties that make a contribution to the unique assignment that will help in the pursuit of its goals or the realisation of its result, in as far as they do not fall under the hierarchy of the organisation underwriting the assignment. Those who do not, in the operational sense, fall under the control of the principal or the assignment leader also belong to this category. Both sister organisations and autonomous third parties can also be regarded as belonging to this group.

The involvement of input providers can vary greatly for each unique assignment. On the scale of involvement, suppliers or input providers can be put between the two extremes of 'anonymous' and 'co-maker' (see Figure 5.3). On another scale, 'universal' is at one end and 'specific' at the other. If these two scales are combined, four categories of involved parties can be distinguished, as shown in the figure. A specific organisation that supplies input can, in the course of the unique assignment, belong to more than one of these categories.

Involvement / Supply	Anonymous	Co-maker
Universal	The corner shop	The contractor
Specific	The research institute	The architect

5.3   Categorisation of input providers

In the corner shop, everyone can buy what is available. Nobody is interested in what the buyer plans to do with his purchase, and the buyer does not usually care who made the article. This is the easiest type of involvement for every unique assignment and requires the least attention.

In the case of contractors, matters are less simple. Whether they are from the construction sector, the installation sector, computerisation, reorganisation or policy, contractors are known individually for each unique assignment and, if all goes well, they supply exactly what has been agreed. Because it is possible to choose universally applicable elements for a unique assignment from a number of equally qualified contractors, great care must be taken to select the best.

The eminent and independent character of research institutes is often an argument for involving such an institute in a unique assignment. It is frequently a question of getting the best possible contribution to the assignment where, beforehand, it is not possible to specify the output in detail. The reputation of the supplier must then act as a guarantee, especially in regard to independence. What must be achieved is then not what one of the parties involved considers to be the best course of action, but what is best in relation to the result or the goals.

'Co-makership' is more complicated for the architects (designers, policy makers and engineers) than it is for the contractors. The architect is often the one who must specify the desired outcome in terms of goals, external interfaces, requirements or wishes, but, even more often, he must devise the solutions that best meet the aims that have been set for the required outcome specifications.

Assignment team members

To begin with, the group known as 'assignment team members' includes all those who, in - at least - the operationel sense, are subordinate to the assignment leader of a unique assignment. In addition, this group also includes those who are also functional subordinates of the assignment leader and those who have a hierarchical responsibility to report to him.

Output users

In projects, and even more in programmes, there are many parties who are confronted with the outcomes. There can be subtle distinctions when using the word 'use', which can vary from 'At last I am going to get what I have wanted for so long', to 'Everything that I have been aiming at for so long has been destroyed'. It is therefore not only the satisfied users that fall into this category but also the angry, frustrated 'victims'. As well as these two extremes, there are other groups. These are often intermediary groups who can or may act on behalf of the final users or the victims.

The test group is a body that is often employed by the principal, on the user's behalf, to make sure that the outcome is useable. A group delegated to guard users' interests sometimes represents them from the very beginning of a unique assignment. For some very large and, therefore, frequently anonymous user groups, the marketing department often acts as their representative. Sometimes use is made of citizen or user panels that are consulted for various projects or programmes.

The keepers and the maintainers or 'upkeepers' of the outcomes of the unique assignment are the final two categories of output users. Sometimes, these are the owners. The keepers are those who must always know what there is, where it is and whose it is. The maintainers are the people who must take preventive or corrective measures to maintain the outcomes. A special group of maintainers can be formed to destroy the outcomes of the project result as soon as they are no longer required.

It is obvious that a player in a particular unique assignment can belong to more than one category at the same time. For example, on the one hand, a supplier can supply goods without knowing much about what they are used for and, on the other hand, he can be the possible source of capacity for a programme's critical success effort. Without the contribution of this 'co-maker', the programme cannot be successfully concluded.

Wherever and whenever possible, all of the players mentioned can and will want to exert their influence on the course of the unique assignment. Some will direct their efforts to exercising a positive or negative influence on the course: smoothing, blocking, showing the ropes, interrupting, creating diversions, misguiding etc. Others prefer to expend their energy on the result or the outcomes: misuse, use, destruction, improvement etc.

Analyse the environment (factors and players)

Every unique assignment has a relevant environment within which a number of factors and players have a role. Most disasters, excluding natural ones, are caused by players. Each factor and player can be important; this implies that influencing factors also influence players.

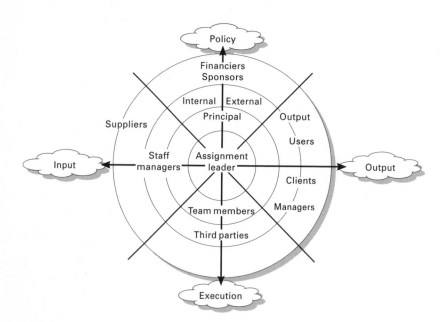

Behind almost every factor there is a player

How to achieve this:

- Identify the relevant players.
- Ask them how they view the unique assignment, their knowledge of it, its clarity, parts with which they agree and disagree and the internal nuances of this opinion.
- Explain any problems or goals behind the unique assignment and ask their opinions on it.
- Discuss with the policy makers to what extent and the way in which the interests of those involved are included.
- Ensure that the players and their organisation make it clear what the priorities are in the (parts of) the unique assignment.
- Determine each player's influence in terms of nature (positive or negative), power, basis (legal/financial/capacity) and interest.
- Analyse existing and potential relationships between the players and estimate the possible autonomic development of these relationships and the players' relationships with the unique assignment.
- Compile an environmental analysis report and set out the consequences of its conclusions in the organisation management plan of the relevant decision document and/or programme plan.

A number of tips:

- Compiling an environmental analysis at the start of a unique assignment is usually worthwhile.
- This analysis will sometimes have to be repeated in the interim, if, for example, there is a significant, unexpected change of players.
- There is always a relevant environment for every unique assignment.

5.2 Determine the failure factors and analyse the risks

Recognising and tracing failure factors and risks in a unique assignment can be done in a number of ways. What is important is that it takes place. Before starting a unique assignment, it is always worthwhile carrying out a failure-factor analysis, sometimes known as a risk analysis. This will help with the timely recognition of future and potential problems. The possible effects of every disruption can be quantified and estimated. In addition, it will be necessary to have a contingency plan (a 'what if?' plan) in place for all the main failure factors. Where risk is greatest, the margins must be correspondingly wide.

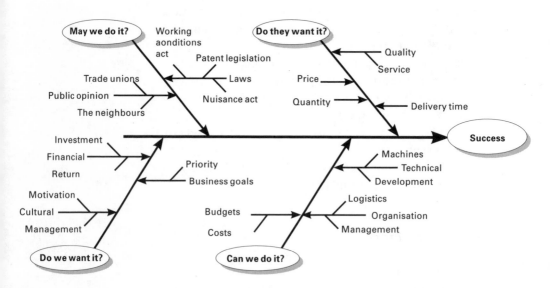

Optimism and pessimism help determine risk assessment

How to achieve this:

- Organise a failure-factor analysis (FFA) involving everyone concerned.
- Find out if everyone has the same picture of the unique assignment.
- Allow everyone to work out for themselves which failure factors could prevent the assignment from achieving its planned outcome, prevent the carrying out of the primary efforts and hinder its management or control.
- Make a list of the jointly recognised failure factors and ask everyone to estimate the likelihood of their actually happening.
- Reach a joint estimate for each failure factor and then determine individually what would be the effects if each individual failure factor were to occur.
- Make a collective overview of these findings and try as a group to find ways of solving, preventing, avoiding or blocking the most serious failure factors.
- Record the final agreements in a contingency plan and control the progress of this plan through the normal channels.

A number of tips:

- The FFA is aimed at ensuring the future of the unique assignment.
- After the FFA, the question 'Are we ready?' should be answered with 'Yes, on condition that...'.
- Do not rush an FFA; this will save you time in the long run.

5.3 Checklist

Develop support

Support for a unique assignment cannot be taken for granted. Support will certainly not be found among those who oppose the goals or the project result. Making a careful inventory of the forces that affect the unique assignment is the first thing that must be done when attempting to drum up support for it.

Mutual interests / Trustworthy	Yes	??	No
Yes	Friends	Doubters	Opponents
No	Coalition partners	Opportunists	Foes

The unique assignment is carried by the support that it receives

How to achieve this:

- Make an inventory of the environmental factors.
- Assess each player's:
· interests
· type of influence (positive/negative)
· degree of strength (strong/weak)
· development possibilities.
- Draw up a plan for developing support:
· who will influence which player when
· in which way, with what
· who brings which players together, for what reason and in what way.
- Carry out this plan, control its progress regularly and review it if circumstances so dictate.

A number of tips:

- The actual outcome of a unique assignment is a function of the factual results and their assessment by those involved.
- Support bases are not stable.
- The principal plays a crucial role in winning and sustaining support.

Communicate with those around you

Communication is one of the most important factors for the success of a unique assignment.

However in practice, means of communication are very often under- or overestimated. For this reason, unique assignments are not always free from tension. One reason for this often unnecessary tension is the complex environment within which the unique assignment finds itself. The assignment is surrounded by people who all want to influence it to various degrees. Communication can make a useful contribution to relieving this tension. It can lead to the creation of the 'right' sort of vision of the unique assignment and offer a basis for understanding, trust and participation.

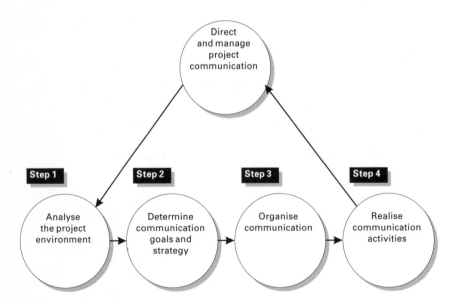

Even a good project or programme can be damaged by poor communication

How to achieve this:

- Analyse the unique assignment's environment.
- Develop a vision of the basic principles and the conditions for communication about the unique assignment.
- Determine the communication target groups, goals and strategy.
- Organise communication:
· divide the tasks, responsibilities and powers
· ensure staffing levels
· determine the communication style, culture, means, channels, systems and procedures, and record this in the decision document's organisation management plan and/or programme plan.
- Realise the communication activities.
- Control progress, adjust ... or replan.

A number of tips:

- A flawed unique assignment cannot be saved by good communication.
- Give adequate priority to communication and recognise its importance in organisation management.
- Be on your guard against the whole exercise turning into a communication circus; word of mouth is often also a powerful communication tool.

184   Working together on unique assignment

6 Working together on unique assignments

Co-operation is necessary to bring a unique assignment to a satisfactory conclusion. We will highlight the process, the interactive side of unique assignments, based on the premise that it is well-nigh impossible to complete such an assignment if no attention is paid to the process of co-operation. And the more unique the assignment, the more difficult this is. Working together and supervising co-operation demands extra effort from all concerned. Those working on unique assignments have no history of co-operation: they have been brought together for this one assignment and will have to find a way of working together. In this type of situation, terms from the 'art of co-operation' come to the fore, such as team building, leadership, conflict management and decision making.

How successfully the unique assignment is carried out depends to a large extent on the assignment leader and the team. Those involved must have more than just knowledge of the subject matter – the chemistry between them is equally important.

Working together as a team

In most cases, the contribution of a number of individuals is necessary to bring about the successful completion of a unique and complex assignment with limited resources. In some cases, co-operation consists of simply keeping each other up to date by telephone, fax or e-mail. In other cases, team members tackle the assignment together. Despite the fact that working in teams is a regular topic of discussion, working with, in or for a team is something that many people would rather avoid. In practice, we hear teamwork referred to as: 'We are not a team, because everyone works for themselves', 'Working together in a team only slows things down', 'Just tell me what to do and I'll do it', 'When it comes to the crunch, the team leader makes all the decisions anyway', 'I am only a researcher, I can't work with anyone' and so on.

The confusion about working as a team often starts at the outset, when it is not clear to everyone what the team should 'be'. When colleagues work together they are expected to behave differently to when they form part of a group around a leader. In the last instance, the only thing that they have in common is the person supervising the group. The group's leader is expected to provide all the energy and guidance, for the management as well as for the primary activities. Just to be clear: the unique assignments dealt with in this book cannot be successfully completed if they are managed in this way!

What is a team? The term 'team' can be defined as follows: 'a group of people with complementary skills, dedicated to achieving mutual goals and who use an agreed working method for which they take joint responsibility'.

For years now, people have been searching for a scientifically based argument that tells us what the maximum number of team members is that can still work productively as a team. As yet science has failed to come up with the answer, but in practice, we have seen that time and time again the maximum number of team members is about 10 or 12. The reason for this is mainly practical. The more team members there are, the more difficult it is to arrange meetings. And, even more importantly, the more team members there are, the more complex the interaction. A free exchange of ideas is only possible with a limited number of people. Moreover, if the group is too large, it is difficult to be aware of each other, in the psychological sense, and the team members have less 'broadcasting time' available to contribute actively to the group.

Strange as it may seem, there has been very little research done into the minimum number of team members. Because team members must be able to take over each other's tasks - teams must not be left vulnerable if a team member becomes ill or leaves - teams should probably consist of at least four people.

The term complementary - in professional ability, in cognitive skills and in team behaviour - is very important for the realisation of the assignment. Professional ability can be broken down into primary competencies in one or more areas that are necessary for carrying out the unique assignment. Cognitive skills can be regarded as the ability to combine information, fantasies, experiences, ideas, opinions and decisions in such a way as to provide new possibilities for team members, enabling them to pursue the goals or achieve the outcome of the unique assignment effectively, efficiently, creatively and flexible.

Being committed

If the assignment leader does his job properly, he will first assess which professional skills and what type of team behaviour (creative, investigative, questioning) is necessary to bring the unique assignment to a successful conclusion. In an ideal world, team members are then gathered together on the basis of this list of ideals. However, in the real world, teams are usually formed in a completely different way: people try to gather together as many of 'our kind of people' as they can ('our kind' in terms of their professional ability, their formal position in the organisation and their style of co-operation), or anyone with time on his hands is assigned and expected to work enthusiastically.

Every team member can be expected to be committed to the task in hand, achieving the project result or pursuing the programme goals. If they do not feel at one with the task in hand, they cannot be expected to put in any extra effort on its behalf. Conflicts are usually more easily solved when those concerned know what they hope to achieve by working together. When there is no commitment, individuals will tend to concentrate on personal, professional or organisational differences, because there is no 'reason' to compromise or look at the matter from a different point of view. Commitment must be to the whole assignment and not just to part of it. It is almost impossible to form a productive team when its members flit in and out of it at will. Naturally, each individual team member is responsible for the commitment of the whole team. The management of the permanent organisation must to a large extent ensure that the conditions are in place to facilitate this. However, all too often team members are taken away from their unique assignment because they are needed for another, more urgent matter.

Finally, there must be a sense of mutual or team responsibility. It is not enough for one person to hold responsibility for the completion of the assignment; the whole team must have a feeling of mutual responsibility. One important condition is that those concerned must be allowed to manage the work themselves and be given up-to-date, accurate information of how their efforts are progressing. All too often, a team is made accountable for its deeds without first being given the tools necessary to carry out the task!

Despite the fact that teams can vary enormously in their composition, goals, previous history and limiting conditions, most teams develop broadly according to a recognised pattern. Team members are faced with various problems during each phase of the team's development. These problems will seldom be voiced, but they can be inferred.

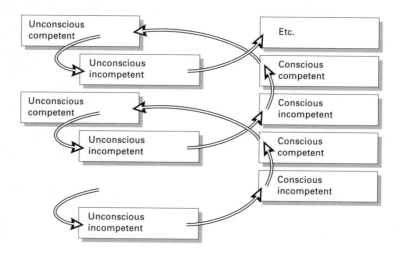

The most important message can often be read between the lines

How to achieve this:

- Don't forget that the following factors are an integral part of team building:
- · looking for acceptance: do they like me, do I belong, what can I contribute? etc.
- · exchanging information: what should or shouldn't I say, what do the others say and not say?
- · integrating goals: what is the project result, which programme goals are we going to pursue, what will this achieve, what are classed as main issues and what are not?
- · tackling and managing the assignment: who's in charge, what are the rules of the game, who does what?
- Discuss problems and bottlenecks as soon as they become apparent:
- · make your dissatisfaction clear
- · encourage and support others in doing the same
- · make a diagnosis
- · stop and think
- · work at being accepted, exchange information, achieve goal integration and manage the assignment.

A number of tips:

- – Spiral movement goes up as well as down.
- – Forming a team is a task that is never completed.
- – A happy team is a hard-working team.

Your behaviour in the team

One of the most important characteristics of a team is that its members interact. People influence one another. You can divide human behaviour into roughly four categories:

- Interactive behaviour is co-operative, working together and offering encouragement.
- Defiant behaviour is being opposed to, being critical of and withdrawal.
- Dominant behaviour is showing leadership and standing above certain matters.
- Subservient behaviour is submissive, following someone else's lead and dependence.

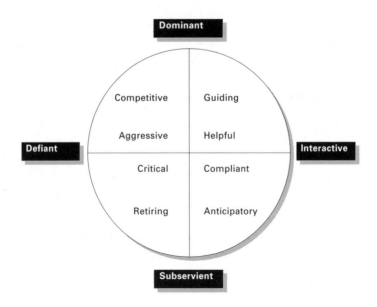

How to achieve this:

– Bear in mind that experience has taught us that the behaviour of one evokes a response in another:
· interactive behaviour evokes an interactive response
· defiant behaviour evokes a defiant response
· dominant behaviour evokes a subservient response
· subservient behaviour evokes a dominant response.
– Try to convince someone showing defiant behaviour to change their ways by displaying interactive behaviour rather than by being confrontational.
– Bear in mind that an effective team requires every type of behaviour. Although defiant behaviour sounds negative, a team must be able to be critical. And it is self-evident that leaders must show dominant behaviour and followers must be more subservient.
– Be aware of the following pitfalls:
· all behaviour patterns are adequate in certain situations; it is not a good idea to thwart each other if you are planning to climb a mountain together!
· all behaviour patterns can degenerate into a caricature; submissiveness is no bad thing, but slavish behaviour must be avoided!

A number of tips:

– Supervision can degenerate into a takeover and helpfulness can become patronising.
– Criticism can often sound negative and injurious.
– Aggressive behaviour is often seen be destructive.

6.3 Make use of team members' individual competencies

Each member of the assignment team has certain qualities and competencies, which we refer to as a team role. It is self-evident that each team role has its strengths and weaknesses. Ensure that you have an effective team.

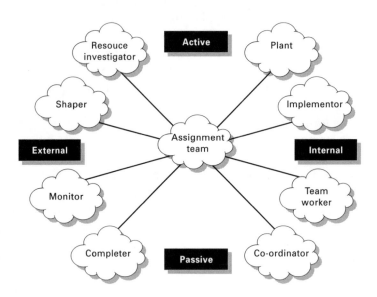

You can lead a horse to water, but you can't make him drink

How to achieve this:

- Ensure that all the team roles are complete, overlapping where necessary.
- Make use of people's strengths in their chosen team role.
- Respect and make use of differences, encouraging others to do the same.

A number of tips:

- Everyone has their own preferred team role.
- Each project phase or programme stage requires a team with a specific mix of roles.
- People can carry out more than one team role.

6.4 Work together

Content, procedure and interaction are the three equally important aspects of working together in groups or teams on unique assignments.

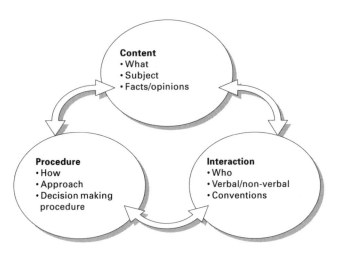

To be able to work together, you must first want to do so

How to achieve this:

– Determine the content:
· what must be achieved and how
· for what purpose the group has been formed.
  For example:
· to determine the goals or problems, result specification
· to clarify the concept
· to exchange information, theories or ideas.
– Determine the procedures:
· how the team will work together
· how meetings will be organised.
  For example:
· decision making processes
· drawing up an agenda, taking minutes
· meeting procedure.
– Determine the interaction:
· the way in which co-operation will take place.
  For example:
· the ratio of listening to speaking
· verbal and non-verbal behaviour
· the way in which we react to one another.

A number of tips:

– Content and procedures can be planned beforehand.
  However, this is not the case with interaction; this
  only becomes obvious when co-operation is a fact.
– This does not mean that the progress of interaction
  cannot be controlled.
– Poor interaction has a negative effect on both the
  content and the procedures.

Take care when making decisions

When someone is confronted with a problem, their first reaction is to 'leap' to one solution. In so doing, they run the risk of being blind to any alternative solutions. An even greater danger could be that by reverting to problem-solving behaviour, our subject could, in fact, find a solution to the wrong problem! You can regard every potential decision as a problem to be solved, but an effective decision making process consists of a number of steps.

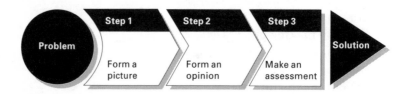

A sound decision is understood and accepted by all those concerned

How to achieve this:

- First, concentrate on forming a picture:
  - describe the aim of the decision in broad terms
  - gather and exchange all available information
  - draw up the decision making procedure
  - monitor this procedure
  - don't even try to think of a solution yet!
- Second, form an opinion:
  - explain the various opinions drawn from the information available
  - formulate the requirements that a solution must meet
  - list the views concerning possible solutions
  - ask everyone's opinion and ensure that the interaction process is completed rapidly
  - don't even try to think of the best solution yet!
- Finally, make the decision:
  - choose from the alternatives based on each other's assessments
  - review the possible consequences and judge if these are acceptable
  - reach agreement about implementing the decision
  - monitor the interaction process, do not overrule anyone
  - now you can finish it!

A number of tips:

- A vague agreement to which everyone assents is not a decision.
- A decision to take no decision for the time being is also a decision.
- The group's decisions can be influenced by 'groupthink'.

Effective consultation

Consultation is very important if a team is to function successfully. Informal, bilateral consultation is often adequate, but consultation with the whole team at previously determined times is essential. Try to reach agreement on this, perhaps meeting once a week.

Talk doesn't get the work done

How to achieve this:

- Ensure that the chairperson is competent. This task will include:
  - preparing an adequate agenda and ensuring that items on the agenda are dealt with according to procedure
  - ensuring that the meeting is adequately planned
  - ensuring that everyone has their say, observing good time management and wrapping up discussion points
  - summarising discussions and drawing conclusions.
- Ensure that people know how to behave in meetings. A good participant will raise points that he considers to be important, listens to others and remains involved.
- Ensure that the agenda is adequate and feasible and, when possible, contains set points that:
  - are known to all the participants before the commencement of the meeting
  - are agreed to by all those present before the meeting gets underway
  - can be amended by the participants.
- If possible, carry out a T(eam) evaluation at the end of each session; otherwise less frequently. This kind of evaluation:
  - makes it easier to give feedback
  - consists of appreciation and points for improvement
  - highlights what went well and what could have been done better.
- List the agreements made during each meeting. Limit this list to actions and agreements.

A number of tips:

- It is better to deal with a small number of points thoroughly than with all of them inadequately.
- Real consultation involves all those who have a point to make.
- Consultation is not necessarily decision making.

Manage conflicts

Even the best of assignment teams experiences conflicts at one time or another. Conflicts can be useful - they can breathe some life into an unique assignment or give it depth - but they can also be destructive, when, for example, the conflict is really about nothing. Conflicts can be major, involving a great deal of fuss, but also very small, a simple difference of opinion during a meeting, for example. Conflicts can be about business (goals, problems, results and resources) or personal, where values and identity are at issue. They can be long-standing and completely bogged down, or they may have only just begun.

Conflicts have negative associations:
– They take up a great deal of time and energy.
– They spoil relationships and the atmosphere.

But conflicts can also have a positive side:
– They can clear the air and get things out into the open.
– They can stimulate creative thinking to solve problems.

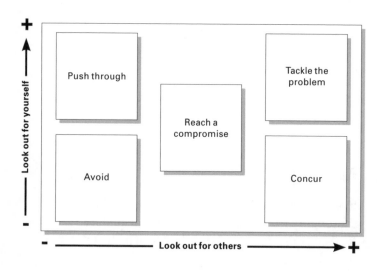

There is no movement without friction

How to achieve this:

- Push through when:
  · time is at a premium
  · you are sure of your ground.
- Tackle the conflict when:
  · you need the others
  · the interests involved are equally important.
- Broker a compromise when:
  · a temporary solution will help
  · the interests involved are reasonably important.
- Concur when:
  · you want to build up credibility for later
  · the matter is of little importance to you.
- Avoid when:
  · the other is clearly stronger
  · your being right solves nothing.

A number of tips:

- Try a different approach sometimes.
- Each approach is only effective in certain situations.
- Conflicts do not always have to be resolved, but they must be managed.

Listen and question further

Every form of co-operation requires communication. This demands two basic abilities: listening and asking questions.

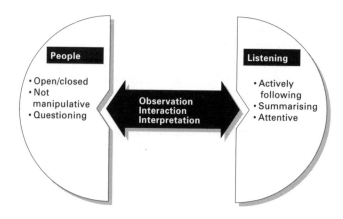

How to achieve this:

- Actively listen:
  · show someone that you are listening to them by giving short verbal reactions or by nodding your head
  · demonstrate your listening ability by occasionally summarising what the other person has said
  · remain attentive and permit the other party to correct your interpretation.
  · listen attentively. Avoid formulating an answer while the other person is still talking. Have an open attitude.
- Ask questions:
  · ask open questions. By asking questions such as 'What do you think?', you will gain the most information. More specific information is won by asking a closed question, such as 'How old are you?'.
  · leading questions or suggestive questions undermine the reliability of information: 'I'm sure you agree that...' or 'I'm sure you're glad that...'
  · continue to ask questions; this is often the only way to get to the bottom of something. Do not be satisfied with a short answer, but get to know who, why and wherefore.

A number of tips:

- Remaining silent also expresses an opinion.
- Suggestive questions elicit suggestive answers.
- Do not underestimate non-verbal communication.

You cannot learn anything from other people without feedback. We can only improve if we hear from each other what went well and where there is room for improvement. Without even being aware of it, we give each other feedback concerning our behaviour and what you say lets the other person know what you think of him or his performance.

Conscious feedback is giving information to someone about how his behaviour is perceived, understood or experienced and what effect it has on the person giving the feedback. It also expresses an opinion about performance. Everyone values honest opinions, appreciation and constructive criticism.

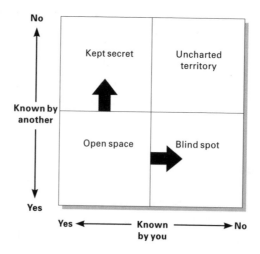

What you don't know does the most damage.

How to achieve this:

- Only mention behaviour that can be changed.
- Do not speak for others, speak only for yourself.
- Speak specifically, do not generalise.
- Describe what you have observed, do not be judgmental.
- Link the feedback to actual situations.
- Describe what effect this behaviour had on you.
- Be aware of what effect your feedback is having on the other person.
- When receiving feedback, observe the following rules:
  - listen attentively and ask questions by way of explanation
  - try not to deny, defend or explain
  - investigate how you can best use the feedback
  - remember that you can always ask for feedback.

A number of tips:

- Being given feedback is not always easy; accepting it is even harder.
- People receiving feedback often take it personally, regarding it as an attack and thinking the person giving the feedback does not like them.
- The whole exercise is aimed at giving effective feedback following generally accepted rules.

Bibliography

Barker,S & K. Barker. *The complete idiot's guide to projectmanagement.* New York: Alpha Books (1998)

Blanchard, K.. et al. *The one minute manager builds high performing teams.* New York: WilliamMorrow & Company, 1990.

Blanchard, K.. et al. *The one minute manager meets the monkey.* New York: WilliamMorrow & Company, 1989

Covey, S.R. *The 7 habits of highly effective people.* New York: Fireside, 1991.

Goldratt E.M. *Critical Chain.* Great. Barrington: The North River Press, 1997.

Harvard Business Review (editor). *Managing projects and programmes.* Boston: Harvard Business School Press, 1989.

Hofstede, G. *Cultures and organizations - software of the mind.* New York: McGraw-Hill, 1997.

Kerzner, H. *In search of excellence in project management.* New York: John Wiley & Sons, 1998.

Kliem, R.L. & Irwin S. Lundin .*The Noah project; the secrets of practical project management.* Aldershot: Gower, 1993.

Kor, R. *Werken aan projecten.* Deventer: Kluwer, 1998.

Landsberg, M. *The Tao of Coaching.* London: Harper Collins Publishers, 1998.

Obeng, E. *All change; the project leaders secret handbook.* London: Pittman Publishing, 1994.

Peters, T. *The Tom Peters Seminar; crazy times all for crazy organizations.* New York: Vintage Books, 1994.

Pfeffer, J. *Managing with power; politics and influence in organizations.* Boston: Harvard Business School Press, 1992.

Revans, R.W. *Action learning.* London: Blond and Biggs, 1979.

Senge, P.M. *The fifth discipline; the art and practice of the learning organization.* New York: Doubleday/Currency, 1990.

Thoms, P & J.K. Pinto. Project Leadership, a question of timing. In: *Project Management Journal*, March 1999.

Weggeman, M., G. Wijnen & R. Kor. *Ondernemen binnen de onderneming; essenties van organisaties.* Deventer: Kluwer, 1997.

Weiss, J.W. & R.K. Wysocki. *5-phase project management.* Reading: Addison-Wesley, 1992.

Wijnen, G., W. Renes & P. Storm. *Projectmatig werken.* Utrecht: Het Spectrum, 1996.

Index

C

credibility 203
criteria for programme management 106-9, 135, 137
    value rating 108, 131, 135
criticism 193, 206

D

decision documents 22, 27, 29-31, 73, 76, 77, 78-9, 86, 88, 155, 183
decision making 16, 17, 21, 22, 27, 28-31, 77, 96, 102, 104, 109-10, 146, 187, 197, 198-9, 201
    structured decision making 24
defiant behaviour 192, 193
definition phase in projects 24, 38, 42-3, 81, 83
delegation 142, 146, 149, 150, 159
    as a leadership technique 165
description of results in projects 17, 23, 30, 34-5, 36-7, 40-41, 45
design constraints affecting projects 53, 83
design phase in projects 24, 38, 44-5
discipline-oriented line of approach to projects 55
dissatisfaction 191
diversification 65
dominant behaviour 192, 193
duplication of procedures 153

E

efficiency 14, 187
    as a criterion for programme management 106, 108, 128-31
efforts *see* activities in a programme/project
emotional involvement 141, 159
empowerment 147
encouragement 165, 192
environmental factors in unique assignments 169-83
    analysis of 176-7
'ER' goals in programmes 114, 119
evaluation of projects 57, 91, 98-9
exaggeration 61
expectations 31, 37, 115
expertise 142, 146, 148, 161, 163
external influencers 171-2

implementation stage in programmes 103, 105, 109, 120-21

improvisation 14, 15, 18, 104, 111

influence 170, 172, 175

information 22, 93, 95, 99, 101, 109, 133, 143, 155, 167, 187, 189, 191, 197, 199

accuracy 189

as a management aspect 22, 27, 31, 56, 72-3, 77, 79, 150

initiative 139, 146

initiative phase in projects 24, 38, 40-41, 78, 80-81

input providers in unique assignments 172-4

inspiration 105, 128

see also motivation

instruction as a leadership technique 165

integration (in decision documents) 22

interactive behaviour 192, 193, 197

interested parties as influencing factors 172

interim results 61, 105

J

jargon 16

judgement of character 144, 207

justification of projects 50

K

key roles 156-7

knowhow 23

knowledge 142, 145, 160, 161, 185

see also expertise

L

leadership 142, 160, 161, 164-5, 192

see also assignment leadership

leading questions 205

learning 99, 153

listening skills 197, 204-5

location-oriented line of approach to projects 55

M

MACIE goals 119

manageability of projects 26, 58-9

management 58-9, 102, 105-9, 128-9, 139, 143-4

unanimity in 140-41

P

participants in project/programme work 139-67, 182
persuasion as a leadership technique 165
phasing of work 17, 21, 22-5, 38-9, 61, 78, 93
    transitions 28-31, 76
planning of programmes 110, 136-7
    adjustments in project/programme plans 26,
    64-5, 71, 89, 133, 146
post-evaluation of projects 98-9
power 28, 30, 31, 74, 77, 142-3, 144, 145, 148, 149,
    150, 155, 163, 183
    balance of 101-2, 148, 163, 166-7
preparation phase in projects 24-5, 45, 46-7, 71, 85
primary activities in a programme/project 23, 30,
    36, 38-9, 49, 74, 116-7, 123, 128, 143, 145, 162
    description 76
    management 59, 67
    repetition of 65
principals in programmes/projects 21, 22-3, 28-31,
    53, 59, 75, 77, 97, 109, 110, 138-41, 156, 157,
    158-9, 170
    involvement 141, 159
prioritising in programmes 125, 134-5
problem solving 141, 190, 202
problems 37, 81, 115, 178, 191, 197, 198
procedures *see* activities in a programme/project
process management 110-11
programmes 13-9, 101-37
    adjustments in programme plans 64-5, 71, 89,
    133, 146
    boundaries of programmes 113, 115, 116, 118-9
    clustering in programmes 102, 117, 119, 126-7
    content specification 112-3
    criteria for programme management 106-9, 135,
    137
    description of results 17, 23, 34-5, 36-7, 40, 45
    functional structural divisions in programmes
    126-7
    geographical structural divisions in programmes
    126-7

The authors

Rudy Kor and **Gert Wijnen** are consultants specialised in project and programme management. For some 20 years they have assisted in the start-up of unique assignments, trained project and programme managers, audited projects and programmes and helped people in organisations to professionalise their approach to carrying out unique assignments.
Both have acquired experience in industrial and service organisations in the public and private sectors.
They have published some 60 articles on the subjects of organisation, management, project and programme-based working and leadership. They are author or co-author of 11 books in Dutch. Gower recently published *'Managing Unique Assignments'*, a sisterbook, in which the authors go into the subject more thoroughly. Rudy and Gert are convinced that the project, as well as the programme approach, are applicable to big, multi-billion EURO assignments lasting several years. But the basic ideas of both approaches have also proven to be very useful in small, teamwork-oriented unique assignments lasting only a few weeks.

Rudy Kor   Gert Wijnen